Multicultural America

Multicultural America

Look for these and other books in the Lucent Overview Series:

Abortion
Acid Rain
Adoption
AIDS
Bigotry
Cancer
Censorship
Chemical Dependency
Child Abuse
Cities
Civil Liberties
Cloning
Cults
Death Penalty
Divorce
Drug Abuse
Drugs and Sports
Drug Trafficking
Eating Disorders
Endangered Species
Environmental Groups
Epidemics
Ethnic Violence
Euthanasia
Family Violence
Gambling
Gangs
Gay Rights
Gun Control

Hazardous Waste
Health Care
Homeless Children
Human Rights
The Internet
Juvenile Crime
Medical Ethics
Mental Illness
Militias
Money
Obesity
Oil Spills
The Palestinian-Israeli Accord
Paranormal Phenomena
Police Brutality
Population
Poverty
Rap Music
The Rebuilding of Bosnia
Saving the American Wilderness
Schools
Sexual Harassment
Sports in America
Suicide
The U.S. Congress
The U.S. Presidency
Violence Against America
Women's Rights
Zoos

Multicultural America

by Meryl Loonin

LUCENT
BOOKS®

THOMSON

GALE

San Diego • Detroit • New York • San Francisco • Cleveland • New Haven, Conn. • Waterville, Maine • London • Munich

To Neil, and to Hana and Jonah,
who are growing up in a multicultural America.

LIBRARY OF CONGRESS CATALOGING-IN-PUBLICATION DATA

Loonin, Meryl.
  Multicultural America / by Meryl Loonin.
    p. cm. — (Lucent overview series)
  Includes bibliographical references and index.
  Summary: Describes the increasing cultural diversity in America, and its effects on American society.
  ISBN 1-56006-766-7 (alk. paper)
  1. Pluralism (Social sciences)—United States. 2. Multiculturalism—United States. 3. United States—Ethnic relations. 4. United States—Race relations. 5. United States—Social conditions. [1. Pluralism (Social sciences) 2. Multiculturalism. 3. United States—Ethnic relations.] I. Title. II. Series.
    E184.A1L664 2004
    305.8'00973—dc22
                                                          2003020667

Contents

Introduction

FROM THE RISING sales of rap music to the popularity of Spanish-language television, from the mosques and temples that have changed the skylines of many cities and towns to the sea of faces on the streets of New York, Chicago, or Miami—the signs are everywhere that America is the largest multicultural democracy in the world, and it is growing more diverse every day. More than a million immigrants flood into the country each year, bringing with them traditions, languages, cultures, and religions from around the world. As they settle in cities and towns across America and become neighbors, friends, and colleagues of current residents, they change the face of the nation. It is no longer possible to determine who is an American by a person's skin color, ethnicity, or religious beliefs. Even the nation's popular culture—the music people listen to, the fashions they wear, the movies and television programs they watch—is a uniquely American blend that has begun to cross racial and ethnic lines. This is especially true for the youngest Americans, those under twenty-five, who belong to the most racially and ethnically diverse generation in U.S. history.

Although the image of the "typical" American is certainly changing, it is not yet clear what impact this will have on the nation's institutions, ideals, and values. America's founders could not have envisioned a country in which Latinos represent more than a quarter of the population in some cities, Buddhists and Muslims live next door to Christians and Jews, and African Americans serve as Supreme Court justices and secretaries of state. The U.S. Constitution guarantees equal treatment under the law to all Americans, but one of the greatest challenges of a multicultural society has been ensuring that this guarantee truly extends to everyone. Many laws and public policies have been challenged or amended over the years to try to make the promise of equal treatment for all Americans a reality. Yet the nation still struggles to overcome prejudice and discrimination against its minority racial and ethnic groups.

Changing fast

In the years since the civil rights movement of the 1960s ended a painful history of state-enforced segregation between

America's founding fathers could not have imagined that African Americans like Secretary of State Colin Powell and National Security Advisor Condoleezza Rice would one day hold powerful government positions.

Students of diverse races and nationalities make their way to class in a California high school. The United States may be the most culturally and ethnically diverse democracy in history.

black and white Americans, the country's racial mix has grown far more complicated and confusing. This is because immigrants of all races continue to arrive in America from around the world. The rate of intermarriage between people of different races, religions, and ethnic groups is also on the rise. With multiracial children one of the fastest growing segments of the population, the lines between the races are no longer clear. To make matters even more confusing, many of the racial and ethnic categories the nation uses to define people have become outdated. America's government, courts, schools, media, and religious and cultural institutions are still struggling to catch up.

Adding to the difficulty and confusion are some people who refuse to accept the idea of a multicultural society. Their vision of America is firmly rooted in an era when the nation and its culture were predominantly white and Christian. These people believe that America is being changed beyond recognition by new arrivals from Latin America, Asia, and Africa, and they are determined to stop the tide of immigration once and for all.

Yet Americans must learn to deal with the increasing diversity within their borders, because even if immigration were to end tomorrow, cultural diversity has already become a fact of American life in the twenty-first century. That is why all Americans have a stake in ensuring that the nation finds strength in diversity and not allow it to deepen the divisions between them.

1

The Changing Face of the Nation

IN THE SMALL factory town of Morganton, North Carolina, the priest of the local Catholic church delivers his mass in English, Spanish, and Hmong, the language spoken by a growing community of immigrants from the Southeast Asian country of Laos. Just north of the towering skyscrapers of Dallas, Texas, the families of fifty thousand mostly African immigrants and refugees crowd into apartment buildings that were once home to white middle-income commuters. Visitors to New York City's heavily trafficked Canal Street find Vietnamese markets, Indian-owned electronics stores, and fast-food restaurants that serve everything from Chinese dim sum to Middle Eastern falafel.

From the great city of New York to small towns like Morganton, America is growing increasingly diverse. Americans today claim a wide variety of racial, religious, linguistic, and cultural backgrounds. In contrast to many nations of the world, such as Japan or Sweden, where a majority of the population shares a common ethnic or racial heritage, America is becoming the largest multicultural democracy in the world.

Defining *multicultural*

The word *multicultural* means "of several cultures." It is most often used as an umbrella term to include *multiracial,* "of several races" and *multiethnic,* "of several ethnic groups." Yet the words *race, ethnicity,* and *culture* can be difficult to pin down, in part because they are sometimes used interchangeably. Race is usually defined in terms of shared physical characteristics, while ethnic groups are said to have traits in common such as religion, language, and ancestral heritage. Culture refers to all of the social behaviors, such as language, art, and religious beliefs, that are shared by a particular ethnic group.

America is multicultural in the sense that it is composed of people of many cultures. There are Americans of every

A Hispanic woman takes communion from a Vietnamese priest in California. America's population comprises people of every race and skin color.

race and skin color. Their ethnic origins are Native American, European, Asian, African, and Latin American. They worship at churches, synagogues, mosques, and Buddhist or Hindu temples in cities and towns across the country. It is not uncommon to hear Spanish in downtown Albuquerque or Hindi in Seattle. The nation's laws and institutions are rooted in western European ideals about democracy and human rights, but being an American does not imply belonging to any particular race, ethnicity, or religion.

Why is the nation culturally diverse?

The main reason for America's increasing diversity is the almost unprecedented numbers of immigrants arriving in the country. The United States has always been a nation of immigrants, yet levels of immigration today are the highest they have ever been in the post–World War II era. More than 1 million immigrants enter the country every year. The result is that one in every ten people living in the United States was born somewhere else in the world.

This tidal wave of immigration stems from changes to U.S. laws that allowed more people to enter the country and abolished an old system of national immigration quotas. Under the old quota system, each country was allotted a specific number of spaces for immigrants. Once a country's total spaces were filled for the year, residents from that country who applied to immigrate to the United States were refused. The quota system had long favored white European immigrants by reserving spaces for countries such as France and Germany even when there were not enough French or German citizens applying for immigration to fill them. Rather than allocating these remaining European spaces to people from other parts of the world, they were simply left unused.

The new system, adopted in 1965, eliminates national quotas and instead gives preference to immigrants with family members already in the United States, to people with needed job skills, or to those facing grave danger in their own countries. The new laws took effect during a time of violence and political unrest in many parts of the world. The

impact was dramatic. Thousands of people began to flood into the United States seeking a better life. Many of the new-comers were not from Europe but from countries in Asia, Africa, and Latin America.

The new immigrants crowd into gateway cities like New York, Miami, and Los Angeles, and usually settle in communities with people of similar ethnic backgrounds. However, many have also moved beyond the major urban centers to the nation's heartland, often in search of jobs. They bring with them customs and languages that are markedly different from those of the country's white majority. For many residents of these small towns, it is the first time they have experienced such cultural and racial diversity firsthand.

New immigrants tend to settle in ethnically homogenous areas of large cities like this neighborhood in Los Angeles's Chinatown.

If current immigration trends continue, population experts say that America will face the most dramatic cultural shift in its history. They predict that around the year 2050 the nation will become "majority minority." This means that the combined total of people who are racial minorities will exceed the number of white Americans. In states with diverse populations such as California, New Mexico, and Hawaii, "the browning of America" (as the nation's racial transformation is sometimes referred to) has already become a reality.

Census 2000: Snapshot of America

Every ten years since 1790, the U.S. government has conducted a massive national survey, or census, that tracks the nation's demographic changes. The federal Census Bureau mails a census to nearly every household in the United States, asking

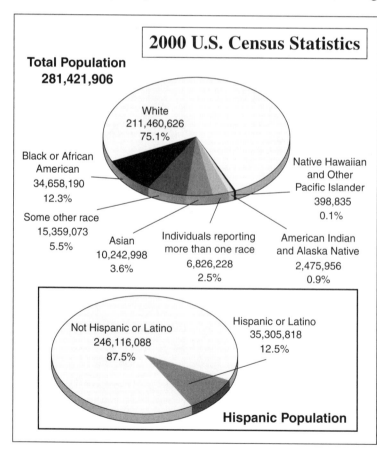

2000 U.S. Census Statistics

Total Population
281,421,906

White
211,460,626
75.1%

Black or African American
34,658,190
12.3%

Some other race
15,359,073
5.5%

Asian
10,242,998
3.6%

Individuals reporting more than one race
6,826,228
2.5%

Native Hawaiian and Other Pacific Islander
398,835
0.1%

American Indian and Alaska Native
2,475,956
0.9%

Not Hispanic or Latino
246,116,088
87.5%

Hispanic or Latino
35,305,818
12.5%

Hispanic Population

Source: U.S. Census Bureau (http://factfinder.census.gov).

Americans to answer questions about the number of people in their households; whether they own or rent their residences; and their age, sex, and racial and ethnic backgrounds.

Inevitably, certain population groups are difficult to count. Minority residents in low-income inner cities and immigrants with limited English skills, for instance, are less likely to have a permanent address and therefore less likely to be counted in the census. Some may also face language barriers when filling out the census forms; others, such as illegal immigrants, may fear cooperating with government officials. Slightly more than 1 percent of the U.S. population may have been missed in the 2000 count, a large number of them minorities. Nevertheless, Census Bureau officials say that it was probably "the most complete and accurate census ever administered."[1]

As a snapshot of America at the turn of the twenty-first century, Census 2000 confirmed that the nation is growing more racially and ethnically diverse than ever before. Yet even population experts were surprised by some of the results. The biggest demographic news of the decade was that the Latino population edged past African Americans to become the nation's largest minority group, roughly 12.5 percent of the U.S. population. In part, this is because Latinos have higher birth and immigration rates than African Americans, but other factors may also have come into play. In 2000, for example, census fieldworkers made the most concerted effort to date to reach illegal immigrants, many of whom are Latino.

Also notable, the census revealed that Asian Americans are the fastest growing group in America. The number of Asian Americans soared during the 1990s due to high levels of immigration. Asian Americans now represent roughly 3.6 percent of the U.S. population.

Another key census finding was that young people under the age of eighteen make up the most racially mixed segment of the U.S. population. Close to 40 percent of these young people are African American, Latino (also referred to as Hispanic), Asian American, or Native American.

The difficulty of counting people by race

It has become harder than ever in recent years to categorize and label people by race because of the numerous ethnic groups that have arrived in America and the way they perceive themselves. The government has responded by adding new racial and ethnic categories to the census forms.

On Census 2000, Americans could choose from among several racial categories, including "White," "Black or African American," "American Indian or Alaska Native," or one of eleven Asian American categories. These Asian American categories reflected various national origins, such as Asian Indian, Vietnamese, Filipino, or Korean. Census 2000 also included an entirely separate question to track the growing number of Latinos in America, since the U.S. government defines Latino (or Hispanic) as an ethnic rather than racial category. This has proved confusing for many Latinos, who do not consider themselves either black or white. On Census 2000, almost 40 percent of Latino respondents checked "some other race" to describe themselves.

Confusion over the Latino question is just one of the problems that makes the census race categories troubling. Arab Americans, for instance, are officially counted as white, and Asian Indians, who were counted as white on the 1970 census, are now considered Asian American. Census critic Nathan Glazer complains, "Many people cannot place themselves in the various categories which require all sorts of manipulations by the professionals of the census."[2]

Interracial marriage and the complexity of race

Counting by race has become even more confusing as the rate of intermarriage between people of different racial and ethnic groups rises, because the children of these marriages identify with more than one race. For the first time in history, Census 2000 allowed Americans to officially check more than one box under the race category. For example, a person with a multiracial heritage might check African American and white or Asian American and African American.

In Census 2000, nearly 7 million people, or 2.4 percent of census respondents, identified with at least two racial categories, and the numbers are expected to rise in the coming years. Former Census Bureau director Kenneth Prewitt predicts that in just fifteen to twenty years, close to a quarter of the American population will identify with more than one race. "I think the multiple race issue is a tremor in 2000 for what is going to become a political earthquake that is coming down the road,"[3] he says. It will force people to reconsider the meaning of race in America.

Interracial marriage is not only changing the face of the nation but challenging conventional attitudes about race and ethnicity. It was not until 1967 that the U.S. Supreme Court overturned the last of the country's miscegenation laws, which prohibited sex and marriage between men and women of different races. Racial taboos against intermarriage remain strong in many parts of the country. Despite

Categorizing Americans by race is especially problematic because the children of interracial parents like these often identify with more than one racial group.

these sentiments, in 1995 it was estimated that as many as one of every twelve marriages in the United States was interracial or interethnic. The number of multiracial children has more than quadrupled since the 1970s. In the words of author Ellis Cose, in just a few decades the nation has become "less 'monoracial,' less black and white, more intermarried and a hell of a lot more confusing."[4]

Religious diversity in America

The census does not keep track of Americans' religious beliefs, but the religious composition of America has changed as well. Immigrants from all over the world have brought a tremendous diversity of religious beliefs and practices to America. "The U.S. now has a greater diversity of religious groups than any country in recorded history,"[5] says J. Gordon Melton, editor of the *Encyclopedia of American Religions*.

Although the vast majority of newcomers to the country are Christian, they are incredibly diverse. Among the immi-

Muslims like these praying in a California mosque comprise an increasingly large percentage of America's population. Islam is the fastest-growing religion in the United States.

grant churches in America today are Latino, Filipino, and Vietnamese Catholic congregations; Korean Presbyterians; and Chinese and Brazilian Pentecostals. In some cities, churches have become what one journalist describes as "multilingual zones": "A single church building may have a Spanish-speaking congregation on Sunday morning at eight, an English-speaking congregation at ten, a Korean-speaking congregation at two o'clock in the afternoon, and a Vietnamese group in the evening."[6]

Churches across the nation have also adopted symbols, music, holidays, and religious practices of special significance to immigrant groups. It is estimated, for instance, that nearly one in every four American Catholics today is Latino. In the Southwest, Catholic churches have welcomed a growing population of Mexican immigrants by adding to their services Mexican mariachi music, Spanish-language hymns, and portraits of the Virgin of Guadalupe, a highly revered symbol of Mexican Catholicism.

While most Americans still associate with some form of Christianity, the percentage of those who are non-Christian is believed to be more than one-fifth of the U.S. population and growing. Asian immigrants in particular have dramatically changed the nation's religious life. Buddhist immigrants, for example, arrive from all over the Asian world, including China, Korea, Vietnam, and Cambodia. Some researchers believe there are 2 million Buddhists in the United States today. Immigrants from India have also brought a thriving Hindu community to American shores. In the past fifteen years alone, the number of Hindus in the United States has nearly tripled as more immigrants arrive to fill jobs in engineering, medicine, and computer science. It is estimated that there are nearly 1 million Hindus nationwide, as well as a growing number of Sikhs (who practice a religion based on the writings of Indian spiritual teachers).

Islam, however, is the fastest-growing religion in America. Muslims, the followers of Islam, are likely to soon surpass the number of Jews as the nation's second largest religious group. Most estimates suggest that between 4 and 6 million Muslims live in America today. The Muslim community in the United States is very diverse. Many Muslims arrive from Asian countries such as India, Pakistan, and Indonesia. Others come from Africa and the Arab countries of the Middle East. There are also many African American converts to Islam; they practice a form of the religion that combines traditional teachings with beliefs established by black religious leaders in America.

The face of American Judaism is also changing as immigrants arrive from eastern Europe, Russia, and the Middle East. Judaism has been profoundly affected by the growing rate of interfaith marriage, which has nearly tripled among young Jewish adults in the past thirty years. For decades, many rabbis refused to perform interfaith weddings unless the non-Jewish partner converted to Judaism or the couple agreed before the wedding to raise their children as Jews. However, a growing number of Jewish leaders have recently begun to take a different stance, arguing that Jews must accept marriage partners of all faiths into their communities. "Any way you look at it," says one rabbi from Cincinnati, "intermarriage is an inevitable consequence of an open society."[7]

In fact, interfaith marriage is an issue that many immigrant religious groups, including Hindus, Muslims, and Catholics, struggle to come to terms with as their children and grandchildren assimilate into the mainstream culture. In schools, social settings, and workplaces, young Jews, Catholics, Hindus, Buddhists, and Muslims regularly interact with people of different faiths. Some of them are bound to fall in love and marry. Over time, these interfaith marriages change the nature of religious practice in America.

The regional character of diversity

Even though rising levels of immigration and interfaith and interracial marriage are changing the face of America, not everyone experiences the nation's increasing diversity in the same way. The census confirms that race and ethnicity in the United States are largely divided along regional lines. More than half of the African American population resides in the South, for example, and more than half of the Asian American population lives in the West. Latinos are

U.S. Melting Pot Cities

Source: University of Michigan, Population Studies Center at the Institute for Social Research (www.psc.isr.umich.edu).

	Whites	Blacks	Hispanics	Asians	Indians/ Eskimos	Metro Population
2000 Census National Averages	75.1	12.3	12.5	3.6	0.9	–
Miami–Fort Lauderdale, FL	36.3	20.6	40.3	2.2	0.3	3,876,000
Los Angeles–Riverside–Orange County, CA	39.0	7.8	40.3	11.5	0.8	16,374,000
Albuquerque, NM	47.7	2.6	41.6	2.1	5.6	713,000
Houston–Galveston, TX	48.0	17.0	28.9	5.3	0.5	4,670,000
San Francisco–Oakland, CA	50.6	7.8	19.7	20.5	1.0	7,039,000
San Diego, CA	55.0	6.2	26.7	10.7	1.1	2,814,000
New York–Northern New Jersey–Long Island, NY	56.2	16.9	18.2	7.5	0.5	21,104,000
Dallas-Fort Worth, TX	59.3	14.0	21.5	4.2	0.8	5,222,000
Chicago, IL–Gary, IN–Kenosha, WI	59.4	18.8	16.4	4.7	0.4	9,158,000
Washington, DC–Baltimore, MD	60.1	26.8	6.4	6.0	0.7	7,608,000
Lawton, OK	62.0	20.0	8.4	3.5	6.4	115,000
Las Vegas, NV	63.1	8.5	20.6	6.2	1.3	1,563,000

concentrated in the states from California to Texas, although their presence is growing in almost every region of the country. Vast stretches in the middle and northern sections of the country remain overwhelmingly white.

New immigrants continue to be drawn to major ports of entry such as New York, Los Angeles, and Miami, mainly because of the desire to live among people with similar languages and cultures. In these cities, they often receive economic and social support from extended family members and friends. Black and white Americans, many of whose families have lived in the United States for generations, typically feel freer to migrate to different regions in search of jobs or improved quality of life.

Population researchers identify close to twenty metropolitan areas in America as being truly multiracial. This means that in these areas there are at least two minority groups that make up a percentage of the population that is higher than the national average. Population expert William Frey calls these areas "melting pot metros," pockets of cultural diversity around major cities. Frey says, "Through inter-marriage and the blending of cultures, each of these melting pot metros will develop its own politics, tastes for consumer items and demographic personalities."[8]

Ethnic pioneers in the nation's heartland

Outside of the nation's melting pot metros, ethnic and racial diversity is just beginning to reach other parts of the country. "Ethnic pioneers," the first racial and ethnic minorities to settle in some towns and suburbs, lead the way. During the 1990s, for example, many Latino and Asian American immigrants moved away from urban, immigrant neighborhoods in search of job opportunities. They found both high- and low-skill jobs in cities such as Atlanta, Las Vegas, and Orlando. Others left to improve the quality of life for their families and escape the crime and violence that plague some inner-city neighborhoods.

The dispersal of immigrants from the major cities has been a slow but significant trend. In parts of the Midwest, Latino and Asian Americans are flooding a region that has experienced a decline in white population. In cities such as St. Louis and Detroit, immigrants have revitalized once rundown streets and neighborhoods with bustling new shops and restaurants. Local officials in some regions have even made efforts to recruit new immigrants. The governor of Iowa, for instance, announced plans to open a string of "Centers for New Iowans" to welcome new immigrants to the state.

In a break from old migration patterns, many immigrants to the Midwest have begun to settle in smaller cities and towns, rather than in major urban centers. Yet many of these small towns are not prepared to handle the newcomers' linguistic and cultural needs. Immigrants who are not fluent in English, for example, may have trouble accessing public services. Court systems do not always provide translators. Teachers for bilingual classrooms are in short supply. And hospitals sometimes lack the resources to provide interpreters to sick patients, often asking children to translate critical medical information for their parents. One Spanish-speaking resident of Madison, Nebraska, complained, "It is hard to find Spanish services, to get legal service or get a good doctor. People when they get a problem with the landlord they don't go to complain, because no one speaks English, and the landlord doesn't speak Spanish."[9]

Despite these linguistic and cultural hurdles faced by the ethnic pioneers, their resettlement has long-lasting consequences. The children and grandchildren of the ethnic pioneers are likely to speak English fluently and become integrated into the social and political life of their communities.

The persistence of segregation

Even within the melting pot areas where the nation's population is racially diverse, segregation is still common in neighborhoods, schools, and workplaces. White Americans are likely to live in white neighborhoods; minorities usually live in neighborhoods with other minorities. White children are America's most segregated group. A recent study found that, on average, white students attend public schools where 80 percent of their classmates are white. Meanwhile, fifty years after the landmark 1954 Supreme Court decision in *Brown v. Board of Education,* which ended state-enforced school segregation, 60 percent of black students still attend all-minority schools.

Some people say that Americans simply choose to live in communities in which most of their neighbors resemble themselves racially and ethnically. Population researchers argue, however, that this does not fully explain the persistence of segregation. They point out that there is a high cost to segregation for many African Americans and Latinos. The inner-city neighborhoods where many minorities live have a greater incidence of poverty and higher crime

Inner-city neighborhoods where minority groups often live have a higher incidence of poverty and higher crime rates than suburban communities.

rates than many suburban communities. Life in these neighborhoods can become a daily struggle, which is not something most residents would choose for themselves or their children.

Instead, researchers point to other factors that contribute to neighborhood segregation. In many suburban areas, there is a shortage of affordable housing for working-class or low-income minority families. African Americans or Latinos may also feel that they are unwelcome in some suburban neighborhoods, at times due to open hostility and racism but often because of more subtle discrimination. They may fear, for instance, that they would attract unwanted attention in these neighborhoods since there are so few nonwhite residents on the streets or in public places. In some cases, real estate agents consciously steer minority clients away from affluent white neighborhoods and toward others they feel are more suitable. When minority residents do overcome these hurdles and move into white neighborhoods in large numbers, studies show that many white residents begin to move out. Once again, this leads to residential segregation between the races.

What does it mean to be an American?

In light of the nation's increasing diversity, many people have begun to question what it means to be an American. They wonder if there are values and ideals that people of vastly different cultural backgrounds share in common and if these translate into a national identity.

Proponents of multiculturalism celebrate and affirm the nation's many cultures as one of the greatest strengths of America. They view race and ethnicity as defining aspects of the American experience and believe it is crucial to recognize all of the cultures that have contributed to

the American way of life. According to cultural historian Ronald Takaki,

> When we just look around at ourselves, we realize that not all of us came from Europe. Many of us came from Africa and Latin America, and others were already here in North America. And others, like my grandfather, came from a Pacific shore. It is not only more inclusive, but also more *accurate* to recognize this diversity. [10]

In contrast, critics of this view say people are so consumed with their separate racial and ethnic identities that they have lost sight of the ideals and values that help define what it means to be an American. The country's national motto, *E Pluribus Unum,* translates from Latin as "from the many, one." Opponents of multiculturalism believe the emphasis in recent years has shifted from "one" to "the many." They say the United States is being torn apart into competing ethnic groups, each fighting to protect its own interests at the expense of all others. Social commentator Linda Chavez writes,

> American culture itself has been enriched by what individual groups brought to it. Yet it is more important that all of us—no matter where we come from or what circumstances brought us or our ancestors here—think of ourselves as Americans if we are to retain the sense that we are one people, not simply a conglomeration of different and competing groups. [11]

Racial and ethnic diversity has become a fact of American life. The challenge for the future is to ensure that the nation's increasing diversity becomes a source of national unity, rather than one of division.

2

America's Racial and Ethnic Tensions

IN THE SCORCHING Arizona desert near the Mexican border, small groups of men stand guard. They are armed with guns, dogs, binoculars, and high-tech surveillance equipment that allows them to transmit pictures directly to the Internet. They are self-proclaimed vigilantes, people who have taken the law into their own hands. They have vowed to stop illegal immigrants who try to make the dangerous crossing from Mexico each day to live and work in the United States. These vigilantes believe that the nation is under siege from immigrant groups and that the U.S. government is not doing enough to prevent it.

The existence of such people makes it clear that not everyone welcomes the changing face of the nation. Indeed, there are tensions and challenges that result when people of vastly different cultural, linguistic, religious, and racial backgrounds live together in one nation under a single government and legal system, and share the same schools, workplaces, and neighborhoods. While some people view diversity as one of America's greatest strengths, others are uncertain or even resentful of the demographic changes.

"Immigrants make life . . . better"

Many people believe that the country should keep its doors open to new immigrants from around the world. They say that America has a responsibility to extend its freedoms to people fleeing poverty and oppression. Just as in earlier generations, new immigrants come to America seeking better lives for themselves and their children, and the nation should continue to be a safe haven for such people.

Immigrants of different cultural backgrounds also enrich American life and culture. Though some of the newcomers are poor or have limited job skills, they often work long hours in difficult, low-wage jobs, and rank high among the entrepreneurs and small business owners who spur America's economic growth. In some towns, immigrants open shops, businesses, and restaurants that offer specialized foods and products. Many immigrants maintain strong family values that also exert a positive influence on American society. In many Latin American and Asian countries, for example, children are committed to caring for and supporting elderly parents and grandparents. Young people are

Many people believe the strong family values that immigrant groups maintain (pictured are a Cambodian mother and daughter) exert a positive influence on American society.

taught to respect their parents and take an active role in family life. These traditions continue in America. "Immigrants make life dramatically better for everybody in the places they come to, not just themselves,"[12] one journalist writes.

Anti-immigrant sentiment

Some people, however, especially those who fear the decline of white America, would like to place strict limits on immigration. Anti-immigrant sentiment tends to be strongest at times of economic downturn when jobs are scarce or when Americans feel a heightened sense of insecurity, as when the nation is at war or under threat of terrorist attack. The increasing visibility of illegal immigrants, and the feeling that they are taking advantage of American generosity, has deepened this anti-immigrant sentiment. Some Americans resent that illegal immigrants gain access to public education, health care, and antipoverty programs without paying taxes and taking on other responsibilities of citizenship.

Nativism, the idea that only people born in America really belong in the country, has been a force in American politics for decades. Today nativists argue that "third world" immigrants—Arab Muslims, Indian Hindus, Africans, or Latinos—will fail to assimilate into the dominant culture. Many nativists would like to place strict limits on immigration or reinstate pre-1965 immigration quotas that favored Europeans over other immigrants. Florida senator Lawton Chiles expressed concerns about the growing Latino population in his own state. "If we do not regain control of our borders . . . I think that within ten years, we will not recognize the United States as the United States we see today,"[13] he said.

Another argument against high levels of immigration is economic. When new immigrants settle for lower pay, they threaten to drive down the wage scale for other workers, making their jobs less secure. Landscaping companies, hotels, restaurants, and farms in some states may be unlikely to hire native-born Americans to serve as laborers such as crop pickers, maids, or busboys since they demand greater pay and health benefits than some immigrants; people who are in the country illegally will often work for less without benefits. For example, in 2000 an illegal farmworker in the United States was paid roughly seven dollars per hour. This was only half the rate a legal worker would earn but twice as much as a laborer would receive in a Central American country, where a large number of illegal immigrants are born. In this way, many working-class people, labor union members, and residents of low-income neighborhoods complain that both legal and illegal immigrants raise competition for scarce jobs and resources.

These ideas led to a strong anti-immigrant backlash in the 1990s when jobs were in short supply. In a poll conducted for *Time* magazine in 1993, 75 percent of those questioned felt that "the nation's current [immigration] policy has got out of hand and the government should limit immigration more strictly."[14] In 1996, presidential candidate Patrick Buchanan rode this anti-immigrant backlash to Republican primary victories in Louisiana and New Hampshire. Buchanan called for a five-year ban on legal immigration and pledged to use every power at his disposal, including high fences, walls, and ditches, to secure the nation's borders. In the mid-1990s, at both the state and federal level, new laws were passed that restricted immigrants from access to public benefits such as education, health care, and government assistance. In some cases, these laws made little distinction between immigrants who were in the country legally or illegally.

A rise in hate crimes

At its extremes, the hostility toward immigrants and other nonwhites has fueled a steady rise in hate crimes over the past decade. Hate crimes are defined as any crime, such as intimidation, vandalism, and murder, that is motivated by bias against a person's race, religion, sexual orientation, or ethnicity.

In 2001 more than eleven thousand hate crimes were reported by law enforcement agencies nationwide. Of the offenses reported, intimidation and harassment were the most frequent, followed by destruction or vandalism of property. Typical hate crimes ranged from physical assault of a young man because of his skin color to throwing a brick through the

home of a minority family to discourage the family from staying in the neighborhood. Sometimes the violence turned brutal. Ten murders reported in 2001 were categorized as hate crimes. African Americans were the most often victimized by racist hate crimes, but multiracial families, Latinos, and Asian Americans were also targets of such crimes.

While there are many organized hate and neo-Nazi groups active in the U.S., most hate crimes are carried out by individuals rather than groups. The Internet has empowered these people to easily connect with people who hold similar views. The Internet also allows young people and others with racist attitudes to explore socially forbidden subjects in chat rooms and message boards without revealing their identities.

In fact, most hate crimes are carried out by young people, many of them under the age of eighteen. "Many people perceive hate crime perpetrators as crazed, hate-filled

neo-Nazis,"[15] says psychologist Edward Dunbar, when, in reality, they are most often young Americans without a history of criminal behavior who see little wrong with their actions. White supremacist groups have tried to boost their membership by recruiting such disillusioned young people to their ranks. In recent years, they have flooded the Internet with racist Web sites and sponsored telephone hotlines, "white power" comic books, and a thriving hate-rock music scene, all designed to appeal to young people who are already sympathetic to their message that the country is being overrun by nonwhite groups.

Hate crimes motivated by religious bias have also increased. After skin color, religious difference is one of the most visible ways in which people in a multicultural society stand apart from the mainstream. Religious hate crimes are often aimed at people with "religious markers of identity," including Hindu dots on the forehead; Jewish yarmulkes, or skullcaps; and Islamic *hijabs,* or head scarves. Especially since the September 11, 2001, terrorist attacks in New York City, hate crimes aimed at Muslim Americans have increased. Despite the calls for tolerance from President George W. Bush and other leaders, one writer commented, "bigotry hasn't been as socially acceptable in decades."[16]

Mosques, synagogues, churches, and temples across America have also been vandalized. In 1990 a Muslim temple in Quincy, Massachusetts, was burned to the ground. The arson followed years of harassing phone calls and letters, as well as angry demonstrations. A prominent local imam, or Muslim leader, recalled, "whenever a sad incident involving Muslims would take place in the Middle East or in any part of the world, people would focus on us."[17]

According to the FBI's 2001 report, Jews are most often the victims of religiously motivated hate crimes, followed by Muslim Americans. Yet few minority religious groups in America have been spared. Hindus, Buddhists, and Catholics and other Christians have all been targeted.

Tensions between ethnic groups

In some places, tensions between America's diverse ethnic and racial groups have erupted in wide-scale political struggles and even violence. Often these tensions are between longtime African American residents of urban areas and other minority groups who move into their neighborhoods in large numbers. Blacks have been in the country longer than most other minority groups, but they still face widespread racism and discrimination. Even with a growing African American middle class, many blacks continue to live in poverty. Some have begun to feel resentful of immigrant groups who compete for scarce jobs, resources, and political power in their communities.

In cities such as Los Angeles, Houston, Chicago, and New York, African American residents have found themselves clashing with Latino and Asian immigrant groups over how to spend limited resources. In cities with large Latino populations, for example, tensions have arisen over funds for bilingual education. Latino parents usually favor bilingual programs for their Spanish-speaking children. In contrast, many African American parents would rather see funds put to use to purchase new textbooks, recruit new teachers, or repair damaged classrooms. Bilingual education is not a priority for them.

Conflicts have also arisen between poor black residents and the immigrant groups who hold economic power in their communities, such as those who own apartment buildings or grocery stores where residents must do business. In some predominantly African American neighborhoods in Los Angeles, for example, Korean immigrants own many of the small grocery and convenience stores. African American customers often feel that they are treated with suspicion by these Korean shop owners, who, they say, barely speak to their customers, except to complete a transaction. Part of the tension between the two groups is simply cultural: In Korea business is usually done without the small talk and pleasantries that are much more typical in the African American community. Black customers may interpret this distant behavior as evidence that the Korean shop owners are mistrustful of them.

Sometimes interethnic tensions linger just below the surface and it takes only one incident to set in motion a violent reaction. In the spring of 1992, four white Los Angeles police officers were brought to trial for brutally beating a black motorist named Rodney King. An amateur videotape, shot from an apartment across the street from the incident, showed the four officers repeatedly striking King as bystanders looked on and did nothing. After seeing the video, many people became convinced that the officers would be found guilty.

Across the nation, Americans were taken by surprise when an all-white jury acquitted (found not guilty) three of the officers of all brutality charges. Within hours, the mostly black residents of South Central Los Angeles, frustrated with the verdict, began a campaign of looting, arson, and violence. With few whites in the neighborhood and police officers almost nowhere to be found, Korean Americans became the targets for residents' rage. The tension

Widespread rioting erupted in South Central Los Angeles after a jury acquitted the officers involved in the Rodney King beating. The rioting left entire neighborhoods in ruins.

between black residents and Korean American business-people had reached a breaking point. During three days of rioting and mayhem, it was estimated that Korean businesses alone suffered more than $4 million worth of damage. The overall toll to the city was devastating—more than fifty killed, four thousand injured, and over $1 billion in property damage.

In the most vivid way, the Los Angeles riots underscored the challenges of life in a multicultural society. Members of different ethnic groups who live in neighboring communities often understand little about each other's cultures, religions, languages, or lifestyles. It is as if several people are playing the same board game but using different sets of rules. When people have such differing perceptions of each other, the world, and ways of doing things, there are bound to be tensions and disputes.

The difficulty of dialogue

With sensitivities on all sides, it has become difficult to carry out an honest dialogue about race and ethnicity in America. Whites, African Americans, and other minority groups often have conflicting assumptions about race that make it hard to find common ground.

In a national study in 1994, pollster Louis Harris found that there was a huge perception gap in the way whites and nonwhites thought about racism and discrimination. The majority of white Americans were convinced that racism in the country had largely disappeared. On the other hand, a majority of African American, Latino, and Asian American respondents felt that whites were completely insensitive to the aspirations of minorities. With such glaring differences, says author Ellis Cose, "discussions about race have a way of deteriorating into efforts to assign blame."[18] Blacks and other minorities accuse whites of being racist and standing in the way of their success. Whites, meanwhile, blame minority groups for failing to take advantage of opportunities or not working hard enough to improve their situation.

Public discussion about race is further inhibited by the fear of offending someone. Many people worry that even the most innocent comment about race issues will be mistaken as evidence of racism. Whites in particular tend to be afraid to express their views on race issues or to ask questions that are bothering them because they fear they will be labeled as racists. Author Carol Swain has observed this process of silence and self-censorship among her white university students. "It is not uncommon," she says, "for white students to preface their comments on sensitive issues of race with statements such as 'my roommate thinks,' or 'my roommate is upset about,' when really they are expressing their own views."[19]

For many white Americans, it is easier to avoid conversations on race altogether. But this too produces tensions. Many African Americans and other minorities perceive this silence as an unwillingness to address real concerns about the problems they face. The misunderstandings, silence, and defensiveness about race issues among different groups make it extremely difficult to carry on a constructive conversation.

Community leaders across the United States organize programs to help relieve interethnic tensions in inner-city neighborhoods. Here, a Korean store owner greets an African American customer.

Building bridges between groups

Despite the difficulty of dialogue, there have been meaningful efforts over the years to build bridges between racial

and ethnic groups in America. Some groups rely less on dialogue and more on collaborative projects that bring people of diverse backgrounds together. Ethnic community leaders have begun to realize that one of the most effective ways to enact change on both the local and national level is to join forces with other ethnic groups. Often they have a common interest in resolving social issues in their communities and find that their concerns are more likely to be addressed if they come together to achieve their goals.

In some towns, community alliances have formed to improve neighborhood schools, clean up polluted areas, build affordable housing, or combat drugs and crime. In the wake of the destruction after the Los Angeles riots, for example, several local groups were formed to bring together Korean, Latino, and African American community leaders to ensure that misunderstandings were not allowed to escalate to the breaking point again. One such group, the Multicultural Collaborative, promotes projects that bring people of different ethnicities together to address social issues such as gang violence, health care, job development, and immigrant rights, which they believe lie at the heart of interethnic tensions in the Los Angeles community.

Another organization, the City Year Program, founded in Boston, brings young people from diverse backgrounds together. They live and work together while performing service in the community such as mentoring children in public schools, organizing after-school programs, or educating the public about important social issues such as AIDS. In many cases, the young people who work on City Year projects also develop friendships that cross racial or ethnic boundaries. The City Year philosophy is that "service is a powerful way to unite diverse individuals in strengthening their communities."[20]

Diversity and tolerance

Politicians and religious leaders in America often speak of the need for tolerance in a multicultural society. Tolerance has come to mean recognition and respect for other people's beliefs and customs. It is widely held to be the key to relieving the kinds of tensions that lead to violent hate crimes or interethnic conflicts such as the Los Angeles riots.

The challenge in a multicultural society is how far tolerance will stretch when Americans are confronted with people whose race, culture, or beliefs are vastly different from their own. The more something is at stake, or the more people believe they are correct, the less likely they are to be tolerant. "It is not something that societies are born with," says foreign-policy expert Mustapha Tlili. Tolerance can only prevail, he says, with "prosperity, education, intellectual curiosity, [and] openness to others."[21]

Tlili links tolerance to prosperity, because when interethnic violence does occur in the United States (and elsewhere in the world), it often begins in communities where residents face difficult economic conditions. People who live in poverty and must struggle to find work, housing, or health care may become resentful of other groups that gain access to the resources they lack. That is why many groups that attempt to build bridges between people of different races or ethnicities believe they must first address the social issues that affect their communities. Tolerance is also tied to education. People are more likely to be tolerant when they learn to understand and appreciate other cultures. Ignorance, on the other hand, is said to breed prejudice and intolerance.

Yet even when efforts to increase dialogue and build tolerance are successful, diverse groups in a multicultural society will not always agree. Community leader Ada Edwards says about her own work in Houston, Texas, to educate and bring people of different races and ethnicities together, "We may still disagree, but at least we'll understand why we disagree and how we can move forward with it."[22]

3

Racial and Ethnic Discrimination

ONE MONTH AFTER nineteen Middle Eastern Arabs carried out the September 2001 terrorist attacks, Boy Scout leader Khalil Baydoun and five Arab American members of his troop were traveling by ferry from Mackinac Island, Michigan, after a long day of bicycle riding. A fellow passenger on the ferry noticed the boys using walkie-talkies and taking photographs of the Mackinac Bridge, and, in the tense postattack atmosphere, he grew suspicious. The passenger called the police, and after the ferry docked, Baydoun and the five scouts were taken to a van, where they were detained for ninety minutes while the FBI ran background checks. When the boys were allowed to briefly step out of the van to watch a parade of trucks decorated with American flags pass by, they heard onlookers shouting "Death to the Arabs!"[23]

The boys were all teenagers who had been born in the United States. They told reporters that they believed they had been discriminated against solely because of their ethnicity. "What they did to us was not right," said Mustafa Hazime. "I feel unsafe in this world."[24] Yet at a time of national unrest, many Americans felt that incidents such as this were a small price to pay for heightened security against terrorism. In their view, concerns for the public welfare outweighed the rights of individuals who fit a certain racial or ethnic profile.

In principle, the U.S. Constitution, together with the nation's civil rights laws (first passed in 1960) guarantee the same rights and protections to all Americans. In practice, as the incident with the Michigan Boy Scouts makes clear, it has proved difficult to ensure equal treatment under the law to members of all of the racial, ethnic, and religious groups that make up America's increasingly multicultural society.

Civil rights for all Americans

As America becomes more diverse, a growing number of racial, ethnic, and religious groups have begun to look to the Constitution and the nation's civil rights laws for protection. The Fourteenth Amendment of the Constitution, passed in 1868, declares that no state may "deny to any person within its jurisdiction the equal protection of the laws."[25] Yet for decades after its passage, judges and lawmakers did not see a contradiction between the equal protection clause and a system of segregation that forced black Americans to the back of buses and into separate classrooms, hotels, and restaurants.

In 1964, Congress passed the Civil Rights Act. The new law abolished the most blatant forms of racism in employment, schools, and public facilities. It stated that no person in the United States could be subject to discrimination "on the ground of race, color, religion, or national origin."[26] Later laws took the nondiscrimination policy even further, extending it to voting, housing, jury selection, and other areas.

The Constitution and the nation's civil rights laws also protect the growing number of religious minorities in America. The First Amendment of the Constitution establishes the separation of church and state and guarantees that Americans are free to worship without government interference. The nation's civil rights laws ensure that practitioners of all religions in America—Christians, Jews, Muslims, Buddhists, Hindus, Native Americans, and others—will be protected against discrimination in schools, workplaces, and public facilities.

The persistence of racial discrimination

Despite progress since the passage of the civil rights laws in eliminating the most open forms of racism, more subtle discrimination still exists. It is not uncommon for racial and ethnic minorities to be subject to discrimination when they

President Lyndon Johnson shakes hands with Martin Luther King Jr. after signing the 1964 Civil Rights Act prohibiting racial discrimination in employment, schools, and public facilities.

apply for a bank loan, shop for clothing, drive down a city street, or decide where to live. Some real estate agents, for example, steer African American or Latino clients away from certain neighborhoods. Taxi drivers in New York City have been known to drive past a black person hailing a cab to pick up a white person down the street. Even shopping, according to author Kenneth Meeks, can be a painful experience. The minute an African American or other minority steps into a

department store, he says, "there is the possibility that he (or she) will be racially profiled as a potential criminal, followed around by a security guard, scrutinized by a store clerk, or just plain ignored altogether by everyone."[27]

Although they have made significant inroads to many professions, racial and ethnic minorities also face continuing discrimination in the workplace. A national commission convened by the George H.W. Bush administration in the mid-1990s found that African Americans, Latinos, and Asian Americans often faced a "glass ceiling" in the fields of business and labor that prevented them from moving beyond a certain level.

The Federal Glass Ceiling Commission, as it came to be known, reported that as of 1995, 97 percent of senior managers of the nation's top-earning companies were white. The commission conducted a series of group interviews in which minorities were asked about the obstacles they faced to corporate advancement. African Americans said "their talent, education, and experience are not valued in corporate America." Asian Americans believed "their superior educational achievements and high performance are not translated into access to senior decision making positions," and Latinos told the commission "they are always being watched and judged."[28]

Religious discrimination

Americans with religious practices outside of the Christian mainstream are also subject to discrimination. References to religion and God are commonplace in American public life. Politicians end their speeches by saying "God bless America." Schoolchildren pledge allegiance to a "nation under God." Public opinion in many states supports the reciting of prayers in schools and other social settings. Yet the conception of God and religion in American public life is overwhelmingly Christian, and some Americans are uncomfortable with religious beliefs and practices that are outside the mainstream.

Many incidents of religious discrimination are employment related. As the Equal Employment Opportunity Commission explains, the Civil Rights Act of 1964 requires that an employer must try to make "reasonable accommodation of religious practice as long as it does not impose undue hardship."[29] Yet the terms *reasonable accommodation* and *undue hardship* are not always clear. For example, one of the issues that is subject to controversy is the right of employees to wear religious dress on the job. Muslim employees have issued complaints against stores such as Kmart and JCPenney when they were prohibited from wearing *hijabs*. Sikh men have sued for the right to wear a turban on a construction job. Jews have sued to wear a yarmulke while on air force duty. In all of these cases, the employees insist that such religious dress is an essential part of their faith. Employers, on the other hand, argue that religious dress projects the wrong image or interferes with a company dress code that is supposed to ensure that no one person stands out from the rest.

Employers must also determine where and when it is appropriate for their workers to pray, or receive time off for religious holidays. Muslims, for example, are required by their religion to pray five times throughout the day. Orthodox Jews and Seventh-Day Adventists are prohibited from working on Saturdays, their Sabbath. In one case in Arkansas, a Seventh-Day Adventist who worked as a computer operator at a hospital asked that he receive Saturdays off to observe the Sabbath. When he was placed on call anyway and refused to make himself available, the hospital dismissed him from his job. The court ruled in favor of the employee, saying that it was the hospital's obligation to make reasonable accommodation of the employee's beliefs.

Religious discrimination at school

In the nation's public schools, there is an ongoing debate about how to treat students who hold a variety of religious beliefs. According to U.S. law, schools must refrain from endorsing any kind of state-sponsored religion but still allow students the right to individual religious expression. This is

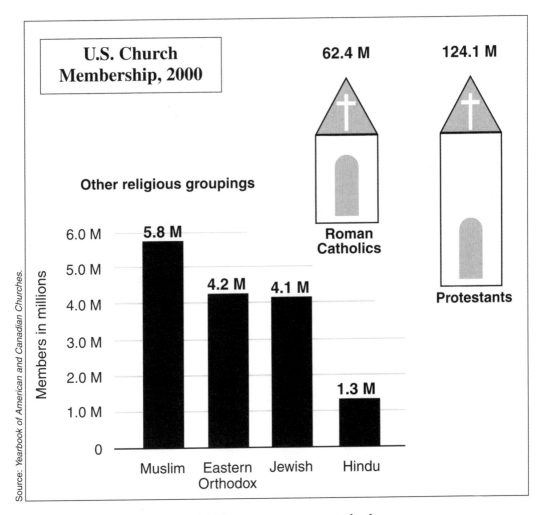

U.S. Church Membership, 2000

Other religious groupings

62.4 M — **Roman Catholics**

124.1 M — **Protestants**

Members in millions

6.0 M — **5.8 M** (Muslim)
5.0 M
4.0 M — **4.2 M** (Eastern Orthodox), **4.1 M** (Jewish)
3.0 M
2.0 M
1.0 M — **1.3 M** (Hindu)
0

Muslim | Eastern Orthodox | Jewish | Hindu

Source: *Yearbook of American and Canadian Churches.*

often a difficult balance. In 2001 controversy erupted when the chancellor of the New York City public schools suggested that Muslim students be allowed to leave classes briefly during their holy month of fasting and praying (called Ramadan) to go to rooms specially set aside for Muslim prayer. Critics complained that special prayer rooms at school violated the constitutional principle of separation of church and state. In the face of strong opposition, the chancellor was forced to back down.

In California, the parents of a Sikh student filed suit against their son's school district when he was banned from wearing a *kirpan,* a small, ceremonial dagger, under his

In 2001 the parents of a Sikh boy like this child filed suit against their son's school after he was prohibited from bringing a ceremonial dagger, a sacred Sikh symbol, on campus.

shirt. The *kirpan* is a sacred symbol of the Sikh faith. Yet school policy prohibited students from carrying weapons, including knives, on school premises. The court ruled in favor of the Sikh student, saying that the school district must make all reasonable efforts to accommodate the student's religious beliefs. A *kirpan* could be permitted as long as it was small, sewn into a holder, and did not threaten the safety of other students.

The practice of racial profiling

The question of what constitutes equal treatment under the law extends not only to schools and workplaces, but also to law enforcement. Indeed, a growing number of racial, ethnic, and religious groups in America have also become concerned about the practice of racial profiling—the use of race or ethnicity as a factor to identify suspected criminals. Racial profiling is viewed by some as a form of discrimination because it singles out individuals based on their race or ethnicity, rather than any specific information that they might be guilty of a crime. Police officers, for example, might stop and search a car for illegal drugs based on the fact that the driver is dark-skinned. Though the officers do not have any specific evidence that the driver is engaged in criminal behavior, they believe that dark-skinned people are more likely to be involved in drug smuggling.

The practice of racial profiling is commonly used in airports, train stations, and border checkpoints, where officials are searching a large number of people for illegal goods such as drugs and weapons. They cannot possibly search everyone who passes through and therefore must make quick judgments about which cars or people to target. Racial profiling is most often directed toward young African American men and women. But Asian Americans, Latinos, and, in the wake of the 2001 terrorist attacks, Arab Americans and other people in Muslim religious dress are increasingly subject to the practice.

Racial profiling captured national attention in the late 1990s after a routine traffic stop on the New Jersey Turnpike ended in disaster. Four young African American and Latino men in their twenties were on their way to a college basketball tryout when their van was pulled over by New Jersey state troopers, allegedly for speeding. The troopers opened fire because, they later told a jury, it appeared the van was backing up to hit them. Three of the young men were seriously injured.

In the aftermath of the shooting, investigators confirmed that the men in the van fit a racial profile of drivers who were frequently stopped on the turnpike. In fact, the two troopers responsible for the shooting had been charged earlier the same year with falsifying their police logs to conceal the large number of minority drivers they were stopping and searching. This practice had been encouraged by their superiors, who believed that minorities were largely responsible for the state's illegal drug trafficking, even though they had no firm evidence to support this belief. African Americans countered that their only offense was "DWB," or "driving while black."

Once public attention was focused on the subject, it became clear that racial profiling was common practice in states across the nation. A federal lawsuit filed in 1998 by eleven black motorists in Maryland, and backed by civil rights groups, charged that Maryland state troopers targeted blacks disproportionately on Interstate 95, a route frequently traveled by drug and weapons smugglers. Like the New Jersey troopers, the Maryland state police believed minorities were more likely than whites to be trafficking illegal drugs.

A study conducted for the case revealed that about 75 percent of motorists pulled over on Interstate 95 were African American, even though they made up only 17 percent of total drivers. Yet there was no difference between blacks or whites in the percentage that was breaking traffic laws. And while more African Americans were being arrested for drug possession, the study found that this was because troopers were searching seven hundred black drivers for every one hundred white drivers. Once the numbers were adjusted so that both groups were searched in equal numbers, it turned out that troopers found drugs among whites and blacks almost equally. The study concluded, therefore, that racial profiling was not an effective tool for capturing more drug smugglers on Interstate 95.

Justifying racial profiling

Whether it is effective or not, many people wonder if using racial profiling is ever justified. As public policy, racial profiling is prohibited under the law. The nation's courts have declared that race or ethnicity alone is not sufficient grounds for suspecting someone of a crime. Yet the courts have also allowed racial profiling when there are facts to justify its use, and when race is only one of a number of factors under consideration.

For example, in one case in the 1990s, a federal appeals court supported a Drug Enforcement Administration (DEA) agent who detained a young African American man after he arrived on a flight to Kansas City from Los Angeles, since there was police intelligence that black gangs in Los Angeles were flooding the Kansas City area with illegal drugs. The man's race was one of a number of factors that made him a suspect. The DEA agent noticed that the man paid for his ticket in cash, whereas most people would have used a credit card or check for such an expensive purchase. He also carried no luggage and seemed nervous as he rushed to find a taxi upon landing. All of these behaviors made the DEA agent suspect that the man was carrying large sums of money from the sale of drugs, and was in a hurry because he wanted to escape detection. Nevertheless, these factors alone might not have made him a suspect if not for the fact that he was also a young black male.

The court declared that the DEA agent was justified in using race as a factor in arresting the man. While large groups of U.S. citizens should not be presumed to be criminals on the basis of their race alone, the court said, "Facts are not to be ignored just because they are unpleasant."[30] The use of race was not only reasonable, according to the court, but it also made for effective policing. Just as the DEA agent suspected, the man was found to be carrying illegal drugs.

Across the nation, police officers have spoken out in defense of racial profiling, saying that it is not racist. These officers contend that it is reasonable to follow young African American males more closely, since they commit a disproportionate number of street crimes; likewise, it also makes

Activists demonstrate against racial profiling in Washington, D.C. Although racial profiling is illegal, American courts do sanction its use when the circumstances of a case warrant it.

sense to stop drivers of Mexican descent at the nation's southern border checkpoints, since they are more likely to carry illegal immigrants or drugs in their cars. Federal intelligence officers have used the same arguments to justify increased scrutiny of Arab Americans since the 2001 attacks, since Arab Muslims are more likely to engage in international terrorism than some other groups. According to law professor Randall Kennedy, many law enforcement officers see racial profiling as "a very sensible, statistically based tool."[31]

The social costs of racial profiling

Despite its usefulness in certain situations, racial profiling carries with it significant social costs for a multicultural society. African American journalist Dan Wycliff explains that the police stop young black men all the time, often for no apparent reason. "A dangerous, humiliating . . . encounter with the police is almost a rite of passage for a young black man in the U.S.,"[32] he says. These kinds of repeated encounters lead to resentment, mistrust, and anger on the part of blacks and other minorities toward the law enforcement establishment. As the resentment builds, it can get in the way of effective policing. Residents of a predominantly African American or Latino community may refuse to cooperate with the police or provide evidence to help solve a crime because they do not believe the police are working in the best interest of their community.

Racial profiling also places a tremendous burden on innocent people. As long as it is permissible to assume that race or ethnicity makes someone a potential criminal, then racial and ethnic minorities, the majority of whom are innocent, will always be subject to questioning, traffic stops, and other unwanted attention from the police. While law enforcement officers may argue that it is only a minor inconvenience to be pulled over briefly for questioning, consider, says author Randall Kennedy, that this person "will be vulnerable not only to one stop but a lifetime of such stops."[33]

In a multicultural society, Americans must consider how much personal liberty innocent citizens who fit a certain racial profile should be asked to give up in order to maintain law and order. They must also explore whether there are other ways to spread the burden more evenly among all members of American society, such as stopping people randomly at security checkpoints, stopping everyone, or using even more informed factors of suspicion, such as behavior or history, to apprehend people.

Combating discrimination: Affirmative action

In the face of racial profiling and other more subtle forms of prejudice, many Americans question how far the U.S. government should go in combating discrimination against the nation's racial and ethnic minorities. Those who have faced discrimination in the past are less likely to hold high-paying jobs or live in wealthy neighborhoods. In turn, their children and grandchildren might not have access to people, schools, and institutions that can open up opportunities for them. Some people contend that groups that are subject to this kind of discrimination should be given preferences in order to level the playing field, and this idea is the driving force behind what is called affirmative action.

Affirmative action policies were created in the 1960s to compensate for past discrimination and to break the cycle of disadvantage that affects many minority groups. There are two main goals of affirmative action. One is to create opportunities for minority groups that might not otherwise be available to them. The second is to increase racial diversity in the nation's institutions and ensure that minority groups are fairly represented. To further these goals, affirmative action programs take race, ethnicity, and gender into account in considering an applicant's qualifications for employment or college admissions. A university, for instance, looking at an African American applicant might examine not only her test scores, grades, and extracurricular activities but also her race in deciding whether to admit her or give her preferential treatment over other students with similar qualifications.

As the nation grows more diverse, there is ongoing debate about which minority groups should benefit from affirmative action programs, for how long, or if the practice should even be used at all. These programs were originally intended to compensate for a long and painful history of racism and segregation against African Americans. They were later expanded to include many of the nation's minority ethnic and racial groups. Today, recent immigrants from Latin America or Asia who have not been in the country long enough to have suffered from past discrimination are given preference over other applicants under some affirmative action programs.

With more groups eligible for preference, some people have suggested that affirmative action programs should distinguish between applicants based not only on their race but also on their economic or social status. The child of a successful African American doctor who lives in a middle-class suburb, for instance, faces fewer barriers to success than another African American child who grows up in a low-income neighborhood and whose parents never attended college. The same argument applies to the nation's

immigrant groups. A third-generation Latino American who speaks English fluently, for example, has access to greater opportunities than a recent immigrant from Mexico, who must overcome language and cultural barriers to succeed.

Critics of affirmative action say such preferences contradict the American ideal that individuals of all backgrounds should be rewarded on the basis of hard work and merit, rather than on unchangeable traits such as race and ethnicity. They believe the nation's laws should be "color-blind" and individuals of all races and ethnic backgrounds should be treated the same way, no matter the situation. Affirmative action supporters counter that idea by charging that, unfortunately, it is not a "color-blind" world, and race and ethnicity still matter. Racial preferences are one of the only ways schools and other institutions can correct for discrimination.

The value of diversity

In recent years, the goal of affirmative action programs has shifted from compensating for racial discrimination to promoting greater diversity in universities and workplaces. A wide range of business leaders, university administrators, and military leaders contend that institutional diversity is essential in a multicultural society. Educators have long argued that diversity enriches the learning experience for all students on college campuses by exposing them to many different points of view. A Harvard University admissions officer explains,

> A farm boy from Idaho can bring something to Harvard College that a Bostonian cannot offer. Similarly, a black student can usually bring something that a white person cannot offer. . . . The quality of the educational experience of all the students in Harvard College depends in part on these differences in the background and outlook that students bring with them.[34]

In 2003 the Supreme Court reaffirmed support for the use of race-based preferences to increase diversity in a case involving the University of Michigan Law School. In its admissions process, the law school specially considers appli-

University of Michigan students celebrate the Supreme Court's 2003 decision to uphold the practice of affirmative action in student enrollment.

cants of certain racial backgrounds in order to increase the diversity of the student body. Race is a so-called plus factor, or one factor among many that makes an applicant to the school more desirable.

Corporate leaders have also spoken publicly about the value of diversity. Senior managers of many large multinational firms argue that a diverse workforce helps them respond more effectively to customers, suppliers, and partners around the world. More than seventy such corporations, including Microsoft, General Motors, and 3M, filed a "friend of the court brief" (a document from a party not involved in the case that argues their position) in support of the University of Michigan Law School's affirmative action policy. In this brief, the companies claimed it was in their best interest to promote diversity on college campuses so that they would have a larger pool of qualified minority graduates to choose from in their hiring process.

Arguments against affirmative action

Although the arguments for greater diversity have growing support in the academic and business worlds, some people believe that affirmative action has strayed too far from its original goal of remedying racial discrimination and creating opportunities for minority groups. African Americans complain, for instance, that businesses and universities use affirmative action to offer spaces to foreign workers or recent immigrants, while groups with historical roots in the United States, such as African Americans and Latinos, are overlooked. These groups still face discrimination in many areas of life that limits their educational and career opportunities.

In the process of trying to achieve greater diversity, schools or employers may also engage in the kind of racial stereotyping that they seek to end. They assume that if they know someone's race, they know how that person will think. African American or Latino students, like white students, hold a spectrum of different political views, interests, and professional goals. Some have personally experienced the effects of racism, while others have not.

To correct these problems, author Ellis Cose argues for a system that thoughtfully takes the totality of one's experiences into account when making college admissions decisions. A medical school, for instance, might consider such factors as where an applicant grew up, and whether he or she is likely to practice medicine in a poor, underserved minority community upon graduation. Cose suggests that this approach does not eliminate questions of race from the admissions process, since race is a barrier that many minority applicants have had to overcome. It does mean, however, that race is not automatically or mistakenly associated with a person's lower economic status or worldview.

In a multicultural society, many people believe this would be a more inclusive approach to college admissions or hiring. They argue it is worth spending the extra time and resources to potentially avoid harmful stereotypes, and the tensions and misunderstandings they can cause.

4

Educating a Diverse Generation

IN 1991 THE school board in Oakland, California, was set to review new history textbooks that had been approved by the state legislature for use in the public schools. The student population in Oakland at the time was culturally diverse—more than 70 percent African American, Asian American, and Latino, and 24 percent white. Yet for years, Oakland's teachers had been forced to rely on outdated history textbooks that included stereotypes and misinformation about the nation's racial and ethnic minorities.

The new textbooks featured the voices and experiences of Americans from a wide range of racial and ethnic backgrounds, and included boxes within the text that highlighted the lives and accomplishments of important African American, Native American, and Latino figures such as Frederick Douglass (the former slave, writer, and orator who fought for the abolition of slavery) and Cesar Chavez (who struggled to improve conditions for migrant farmworkers from Mexico). In the spring of 1991, the editors of the new textbooks arrived in Oakland to take part in an open meeting to which teachers, school administrators, parents, and members of the Oakland community were invited to voice their reactions to the new books. The editors were not prepared for the controversy that erupted.

From the start, the audience was angry and restless. Many people took the floor to attack the texts for focusing too heavily on white Europeans and their ideas. An African

American man charged that the books trivialized the horrible experience of slavery and reflected a racist point of view. Several Chinese American parents complained that their ancestors were hardly mentioned in the volumes on California history. A young Japanese American woman claimed that the textbooks' account of Japanese American internment in camps during World War II downplayed the suffering of the prisoners.

Textbook editor and historian Gary Nash defended his choices. He pointed to examples in the books in which the experience of slavery was covered in detail with vivid first-hand depictions and commentary, and a chapter titled "California in Wartime" that included two full pages on the

In 1991 the lives of such historical minority figures as Frederick Douglass began to be featured in textbooks used in the Oakland, California, school system.

World War II internment of Japanese Americans. "You can't write the history of every ethnic group in California," he later told an interviewer, "you certainly can't do it for the entire country."[35]

Today's school-age children are members of the most culturally diverse student population in U.S. history. The nation guarantees that they will have access to a public school education regardless of their race, religion, or ethnicity, but in a multicultural society, there are many different views about what they need to know and how they should be taught. Decisions about education—from what to include in new textbooks to how to teach children who speak limited English—often result in controversy because so much is at stake. Education helps to shape a national identity, the sense of community that comes from having a shared history, culture, and pride in the nation's achievements, and it has a profound effect on the way young people come to view their place in the nation and the world.

Deciding what to teach

In a culturally diverse society, deciding what to include in a history textbook or curriculum (the content and skills covered in a unit of study) is often a difficult and controversial process. History textbooks are especially controversial because interpreting the past often involves making value judgments about the present. Some people believe, for example, that if slavery and racism are presented as the central themes of early American history, this reflects poorly on the country today. They believe that if the curriculum focuses on the triumphs of national heroes such as George Washington and Paul Revere, it is more likely to instill a sense of patriotism. Others say that even traditional heroes should be seen in all their complexity—that Thomas Jefferson, for instance, was a lifelong slaveholder reflects the moral dilemmas and contradictions of American history on issues such as race.

As students advance through the grades in history or social studies, educators make many decisions about what they should learn. The curriculum cannot cover everything,

so educators must decide which topics to explore in depth, which to mention only in passing, and which to omit altogether. These decisions often reflect fundamentally different beliefs about how students in a multicultural society should learn about the events of the past.

A 2002 report on world history curricula in Wisconsin's public schools, for example, revealed that textbooks used across the state treated Christopher Columbus's arrival in North America very differently. In some, the emphasis was on the disease and slaughter that Columbus and his followers inflicted on native peoples, who were said to have been living in harmony with the earth before he arrived. Another

A painting provides a romanticized depiction of Christopher Columbus's arrival in the New World. History textbooks offer widely differing accounts of the event.

focused not only on Columbus's failures but on his contributions in bringing Western civilization across the seas. A third featured four perspectives on Columbus, two which harshly criticized him and two which praised him for changing the course of world history, allowing students to make their own judgments. Still other textbooks downplayed Columbus's importance and devoted no more than two or three paragraphs to his entire story.

The melting pot approach

Yet for the first half of the twentieth century, most U.S. textbooks and history courses would have praised Columbus's "discovery" of the New World and celebrated the triumph of white European civilization over Native American cultures. This was the era of the "melting pot," or assimilationist, approach to education, in which immigrants and their children were instructed to give up their ethnic and racial identities in order to be accepted (or melt) into the dominant national culture. Having a strong ethnic identity, such as Italian, Jewish, Chinese, or Puerto Rican, was widely believed to undermine the national spirit of patriotism.

In practice, the melting pot often forced children to turn away from the languages and customs of their families and home lives so that they could achieve social and economic success in the mainstream culture. (African American students were segregated in separate schools at this time and not considered by the white majority as part of the melting pot.) Education for all students centered on white, western European culture, and history and social studies textbooks traced the political and military deeds of great leaders, almost all of whom were white. Textbooks were filled with negative stereotypes or misconceptions about people of other races. Native Americans, for example, were often depicted as "noble savages" who were bloodthirsty or childlike. They were rarely considered real human beings who acted on their own judgments and values. In other cases, textbooks omitted the contributions or experiences of non-white cultures and people altogether.

In the 1960s and 1970s, it became clear to many educators that this approach did not address the needs of many of the nation's schoolchildren. The Vietnam War, the struggle for civil rights for black Americans, and the women's movement created an atmosphere of political and social upheaval in the country. New immigration laws also took effect in the late 1960s, drawing people to America from around the world. Many historians began to write social histories that focused not on the people in power but on the lives and experiences of ordinary citizens, including women, former slaves, laborers, and immigrants. Educators were no longer satisfied with a curriculum that focused almost entirely on white western European culture. They began to look for other approaches that would be more inclusive of the nation's minority racial and ethnic groups.

Multiculturalism and education

Some educators suggest that the content of the curriculum should reflect America's diversity. The term *multiculturalism* has also come to refer to an educational philosophy that ensures that America's diverse racial, ethnic, and cultural groups receive recognition and respect. In the multiculturalist view, there is as much to learn about America's past from the lives of unknown slaves and soldiers during the revolutionary period as from the biography of George Washington. A multicultural curriculum stresses that many groups have profoundly influenced the national culture, including immigrants, Native Americans, and African Americans, and their stories are a vital part of the American experience. Historian Ronald Takaki says, "The intellectual purpose of multiculturalism is a more accurate understanding of who we are as Americans."[36]

A multicultural curriculum also teaches that American history is complex. Students must examine not only America's triumphs but also its flaws, including the persistence of racism and discrimination. Multiculturalists suggest that an educated citizen is someone who can see the world from multiple perspectives. They believe this is the most effective way to prepare young people for the future in a globally interconnected world in which they will have to work together across cultural, racial, and class lines.

Does multiculturalism distort American history?

Multiculturalists believe that history textbooks should highlight the key contributions immigrant groups have made to American society.

The multiculturalist approach has come under attack in recent years for distorting American history and culture. Students in a multicultural curriculum are discouraged from criticizing other cultures or judging one culture superior to any other. The problem with this is that some cultures, both

white and nonwhite, are known to be oppressive. Some deny their citizens basic human rights and freedoms, such as the right to speak freely or criticize their government. Others do not permit women or minorities to attend school or participate in the political process. Yet critics of multiculturalism say that the only culture that is heavily criticized in many multicultural accounts is that of white Europeans.

In some cases, multicultural histories are said to be created in response to pressure from the nation's minority racial and ethnic groups, rather than on the basis of historical scholarship. In 1989, for example, a New York State task force proposed a new "curriculum of inclusion" after minority groups charged that the state's history curriculum did not address the needs of minority children, who made up close to one-third of the public school population. In the proposed curriculum, critics recount, white Europeans were held collectively responsible for racism and slavery throughout the world, despite the fact that people of every racial group have committed terrible crimes against humanity. All whites were referred to as Anglo Saxons and WASPs (White Anglo-Saxon Protestants). Students were discouraged from using the word *slaves;* they would be taught to use the term *enslaved persons* instead. There was also little mention of ethnic conflict or oppression among nonwhite groups.

Bilingual education

As American society becomes more culturally diverse, there is growing debate not only over curriculum content, but how to teach it. Many recent immigrants arrive in the public schools with limited English skills. Before they can be exposed to American history or literature, they must first master the English language. In ethnically diverse states such as California and New York, at least 20 percent of students are nonnative English speakers. Many live in homes where no one speaks English well. These children have little chance of continuing their education or gaining entry into the workplace if they fail to master English at school.

Bilingual education is an educational approach in which students receive instruction in both English and their native language. It is seen as a way to ease children's transition into English-language classes by ensuring that they receive the instruction they need in their native language until they can gain English proficiency. Bilingual programs were first implemented in the late 1960s and 1970s to help Spanish-speaking students gain equal access to a public school education. They remained voluntary until the mid-1970s, when the Supreme Court ruled in favor of eighteen hundred Chinese American students in the San Francisco area who claimed they were being denied access to an equal education because of their limited English skills. Following this ruling, schools were ordered to take the necessary steps to establish bilingual programs in students' native languages (if the school had twenty or more students with a primary language other than English). The goal was still to prepare students to move into regular English-language classrooms, but they were also encouraged to preserve their native languages and cultures.

As more immigrants flooded into the country, the number of bilingual programs grew. Many people began to feel uncomfortable with the use of increasing federal and state dollars to pay for students to maintain languages other than English. Indeed, in recent years, bilingual education has come under attack for encouraging immigrants to remain separate from the dominant culture by not learning English. Groups such as the national lobbying organization English First have launched successful nationwide campaigns to end bilingual programs. These groups contend that rearing children in another language shuts doors and creates "language ghettos" in which all of the students in a class are members of the same racial or ethnic group. Immigrant children, they say, should be moved into the mainstream as soon as possible if they are to become productive citizens.

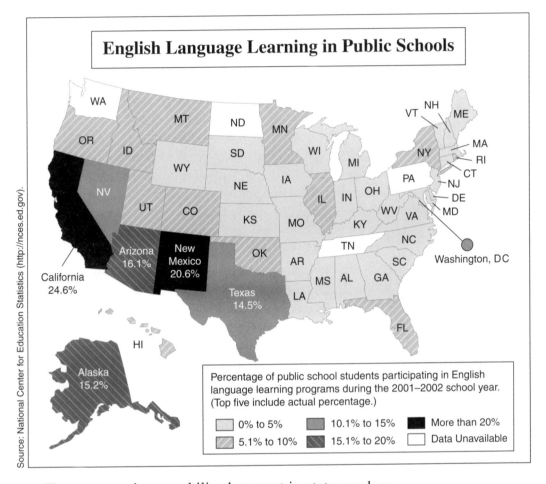

English Language Learning in Public Schools

Percentage of public school students participating in English language learning programs during the 2001–2002 school year. (Top five include actual percentage.)

- 0% to 5%
- 5.1% to 10%
- 10.1% to 15%
- 15.1% to 20%
- More than 20%
- Data Unavailable

California 24.6%
Arizona 16.1%
New Mexico 20.6%
Texas 14.5%
Alaska 15.2%
Washington, DC

Source: National Center for Education Statistics (http://nces.ed.gov).

These groups have mobilized support in states such as California, Colorado, and Massachusetts for public referendums that force schools to place nonnative English-speaking children into classrooms where they are taught to read, write, and speak English. Students are permitted to stay in these English-immersion classes for one year, until they are assigned to regular classes where teaching of all academic subjects is conducted only in English. Social critic Linda Chavez writes in support of such programs that immigrant children "will have to learn English well enough to study history in English, to take college entrance exams in English, to find jobs when they complete school. Wouldn't it be better to give them an entire day's instruction in English?"[37]

Some educators have spoken out against the English-immersion approach, saying that it fails to take into account what is known about how children learn. They believe that instruction must be tailored to meet the needs of immigrant children who arrive with diverse backgrounds and levels of education. With only a year of English and little support at home (where parents may not speak any English), some students may be poorly equipped to face the mainstream curriculum. In their view, mandatory one-year English-immersion programs punish children who may simply need more time to learn.

Preventing hate and prejudice

Some educators stress that the public schools must ensure not only that students of diverse languages and cultural backgrounds receive a quality education, but also that they learn to live and work together with tolerance and respect. They believe that schools should address racism and prejudice directly through programs designed to prevent hate. They point out that teenagers and young adults account for a large portion of the country's hate crimes as both perpetrators and victims. Hate-motivated behaviors such as racial slurs, harassment, intimidation, or graffiti often surface at school on playgrounds and in cafeterias, or in classroom interactions between students.

In schools across the nation, educators have developed lesson plans and activities that help children understand the effects of prejudice and stereotyping and think about how they can respond to them. One such program in New Jersey, Project PRIDE, was formed in response to bias incidents against African Americans, Latinos, and Jews in the state. Students participate in conversations and group exercises that help them find nonviolent solutions to intergroup conflicts. In this program, teachers and parents undergo the training along with the students. In Los Angeles, a similar curriculum for middle and high school students called Healthy Relations not only emphasizes the ways students can learn to resolve conflicts but also teaches them how to recognize stereotypes and negative portrayals of ethnic and racial groups in the media, and not allow themselves to be persuaded by these images.

Other programs address hate and prejudice by asking students to reflect on racist incidents of the past. The nonprofit group Facing History and Ourselves, for example, works with schools across the country on a curriculum that focuses on historical experiences of collective violence and hatred, such as the Holocaust (during which the Nazis killed 6 million Jews, as well as millions more Gypsies, homosexuals,

Certain educators design lesson plans and activities to teach students of varied cultures and backgrounds to live and work together harmoniously.

disabled people, and others). It helps students examine their own attitudes and the moral choices they will have to make in their lives. An important aspect of this curriculum is teaching students about the dangers of apathy and indifference. They learn that, throughout history, people of all races and ethnic groups have resisted hate and that individuals have made a difference in changing attitudes.

Programs such as Facing History help students feel comfortable asking questions and engaging in open dialogue about racial and ethnic differences. The goal, educators say, is for students to begin to recognize prejudice and learn to deal with it, before they form racist attitudes that may become lifelong.

5

Media and Popular Culture in a Multicultural Society

THE LEAD ACTORS of the television show *The Brothers Garcia* are gathered around one of the show's main sets, the kitchen table of a suburban home in San Antonio, Texas, discussing the events of the day. In the show, mother Sonia Garcia is a beautician. Father Ray Garcia is a history professor. The four Garcia children argue, dream about becoming astronauts, fall in love, and sometimes get grounded. But unlike other television families, the Garcias are also devoutly Catholic, keep salsa on the breakfast table, and watch *telenovelas,* or Mexican soap operas, on Spanish-language television. *The Brothers Garcia,* which premiered on the Nickelodeon cable channel in the summer of 2000, is the first American television sitcom to profile a middle-class Latino family. It has proven popular with young viewers from a wide range of cultural backgrounds. Yet executives of all the major television networks turned down the idea for *The Brothers Garcia.* They told the show's creator that mainstream viewers were not ready to accept a sitcom about Latino family life.

America's media and popular culture have a mixed record when it comes to portraying the nation's increasingly multicultural population. On the one hand, racial barriers have been broken down and America's diversity has been reflected as never before; on the other hand, harmful

The cast of The Brothers Garcia, *a popular television sitcom, helps break down racial barriers by portraying characters from a middle-class Latino family.*

or outdated stereotypes have been promoted. "The media and pop culture," says author Farai Chideya, "have such a tremendous power in our society because we use them to tell us what the rest of the society is like, and how we should react to it."[38] For many Americans, exposure to people of other races and ethnic backgrounds is mainly through media and entertainment. That is why popular culture images—from rap stars to sitcom characters to the new multicultural Barbies and GI Joes—can both change attitudes *and* reinforce the stereotypes of the past.

Diverse casting

In recent years, some movies and television programs have helped to break down racial and ethnic stereotypes by casting minority actors in prominent roles that would have once been reserved for whites. African American actors, and to a lesser extent other minorities, play judges, surgeons, lawyers, police detectives, and even fantasy roles such as angels on many dramatic series. Today, few people are surprised to see a black emergency room doctor or judge on a TV drama. Yet only twenty years ago, African American actors who landed parts in major series were often typecast as villains or failures, or limited to situation comedies with all-black casts. Diverse casting, without regard to race, was practically unthinkable in America.

Hollywood movies have also recently begun to feature a rising number of black actors in starring roles. For years, African Americans were cast as stereotypical characters such as villains or sidekicks, but now they often play roles with a greater range of artistic possibility. In part, this reflects a growing trend toward casting black and other minority actors in parts for which their racial or ethnic backgrounds are only incidental to the plot of the film. Critically acclaimed African American actors such as Denzel Washington and Angela Bassett have said that they often look for parts that are not conceived with blacks in mind, because these tend to be more complex and interesting characters to play.

Reinforcing stereotypes

Yet even as African Americans land high-profile parts in some movies and television shows, racial minorities are still often subject to stereotypes and negative portrayals. A 1998 survey by the nonprofit group Children Now revealed that children of all races are more likely to associate positive characteristics such as "having lots of money, being well-educated, being a leader, doing well in school, and being intelligent" with white characters on television, and associate negative characteristics such as "breaking the law, having a hard time financially, being lazy, and acting goofy . . . with minority characters."[39]

Many critics point to TV news as one of the worst media offenders when it comes to reinforcing racial and ethnic stereotypes. African Americans, they say, are likely to appear in stories on crime and celebrities, but not in other kinds of news. "Anyone who tries to imagine African American life from media accounts," says Chideya, "will get the high end (Oprah Winfrey and Michael Jordan) and too often, the low end (crime and welfare), but will miss the middle,"[40] the vast majority of middle-class black Americans who lead normal, productive lives.

At the same time, Americans who are neither black nor white are less likely to be seen in television shows and movies at all. Latinos are the largest minority group in the United States, yet they made up only 4 percent of regular prime-time characters on network television in 2002. When Latino actors do appear, they are often cast as victims, maids, or criminals. Even in shows set in California cities such as Los Angeles or San Francisco, where Latinos represent more than a third of the population, there are few Latino faces anywhere to be seen.

Asian Americans face a different set of challenges that limit the roles they play in television and movies. Despite their growing presence in many parts of the country, non-Asians often perceive Asians' names and facial features as foreign looking. Ming-Na, the Chinese American actress who plays Dr. Deb Chen on the emergency room drama *ER,* says, "People still ask me where I'm from. . . . I grew up in Pittsburgh."[41] During the 1999–2000 television season, there were only seven Asian American actors who could be seen regularly on prime-time network series. Asian Americans are rarely cast even for minor background parts such as waiters or patients. This is true regardless of the show's setting. Several recent television programs that take place in San Francisco, where people of Asian heritage make up close to 30 percent of the population, include few recurring Asian characters. "The challenge," says the director of one Asian American media group, "is to get to a point where our faces and our names are accepted as being American."[42]

Asian American actors like ER's Ming-Na face the unique challenge of being perceived as too foreign to be considered for many mainstream acting roles.

Music that crosses racial and ethnic boundaries

In the music industry, racial and ethnic barriers have begun to fall faster than in movies and television. Indeed, much of today's popular music is performed by African American artists and enjoyed by Americans of all races and backgrounds. The growing appeal of rap and hip-hop, especially among young people, is largely responsible for dramatic changes in the way the music industry in America markets and sells its hottest recordings and stars. Hip-hop music is rooted in the black, urban American experience, but its commercial success is based on selling hit songs to young fans of all races. Sixty percent of hip-hop music sales are to white listeners, many of them in the suburbs.

From rural Indiana to New York City, hip-hop is defining youth culture. Even kids in the smallest towns of the nation's heartland watch rappers on TV. They shop for hip-hop fashions—from hooded sweatshirts and athletic suits to gold-plated belt buckles and jewelry—at the local mall or through mail order catalogs. With Internet access, they chat with fellow fans across the country. Hip-hop culture has also begun to appear in the mainstream media, from commercials to hit movies. MTV, one of the most powerful media outlets for setting music and fashion trends, has been an important force in hip-hop's widespread appeal. Many of the music videos shown on MTV feature black hip-hop artists, even though blacks make up only 13 percent of the station's viewers.

The widespread success of hip-hop marks the first time that black music made by black artists to reflect their lives and experiences has come to define the mainstream in popular music. In October 2003, for the first time in the fifty-year history of the Billboard charts that track the overall sales and airplay of American pop music, all of the top ten songs in the country were recordings by black hip-hop artists.

Sports in multicultural America

While African American recording artists have redefined the mainstream in popular music, nonwhite athletes have changed the face of American sports. African American, Latino, and Asian American athletes have become increasingly visible as the all-American heroes that fans follow on and off the nation's courts, fields, and diamonds—Pedro Martinez and Sammy Sosa in baseball, Shaquille O'Neal and Michael Jordan in basketball, Michelle Kwan and Kristi Yamaguchi in figure skating, Venus and Serena Williams in tennis, and Tiger Woods in golf. These are just some of the nonwhite athletes who have continued to break down barriers. They give young people from suburban Little League fields to inner-city basketball courts something to dream about.

Today, most Americans are accustomed to the fact that African American players dominate many professional

The mainstream popularity of rap and hip-hop artists like Ludacris has helped break down racial barriers in the music industry.

Baseball has become a multicultural sport. Nearly 20 percent of the sport's athletes are Latino, including Pedro Martinez (left) and Nomar Garciaparra (right).

basketball teams. Yet less than twenty years ago, at a time when the National Basketball Association (NBA) was not as financially successful as it is today and television ratings were declining, some sportswriters suggested that white fans would never be interested in rooting for teams that were mostly black. Indeed, NBA commissioner David Stern recalls a time in the mid-1980s "when we couldn't sell ad time, and people would say privately that their clients [advertisers] didn't want to buy into a 'black' sport."[43]

In order to win over fans and revive the league, the NBA began to promote some of the league's star players, making sure fans were familiar with their faces and personal stories. Stern was convinced that the league could overcome racial barriers if people had a personal stake in seeing their favorite champions play and win. The decision to use this strategy of marketing individual players coincided with the height of a rivalry between two popular stars, the Boston Celtics' Larry Bird and the Los Angeles Lakers' Magic Johnson, and the rookie year of a phenomenal young African American athlete named Michael Jordan. The NBA soon became a hugely successful enterprise among fans of all races.

Baseball, the "all-American pastime," has also become a multicultural sport. On opening day of the 2001 season, nearly 20 percent of the players in the major league lineups were Latino. Most of the teams regularly send scouts to the Dominican Republic, Puerto Rico, Mexico, and even Cuba to search for new talent. Some maintain baseball academies in these countries to nurture young players. In countries with high rates of unemployment and dire poverty, baseball is seen as one of the few roads to a better life. "The sport is big in the Dominican Republic because there are no more paths with the same opportunities," says Boston Red Sox pitching ace Pedro Martinez. "Maybe that makes us hungrier to play."[44] Players like Martinez who make it to the majors often retain ties to their native land, pumping money back into their old neighborhoods and sending shipments of baseballs and equipment.

Racist attitudes in sports

Despite these gains, obstacles for minorities in the sports world remain on and off the field. Even in sports that are dominated by nonwhite players, team coaches and managers are still usually white. Many of the Major League Baseball clubs have only begun to address the problem of discriminatory hiring practices that ensure that most of the top management jobs go to whites.

Stereotypes also remain on the field. Minority athletes are sometimes steered away from positions that are believed to

Advertisers wanting to market products to America's multicultural consumers recognize the benefits of featuring minorities in ads like this one for automobiles.

involve leadership or thinking skills, such as quarterbacks in football. In the late 1980s, *Boston Globe* columnist Derek Jackson kept a record of the adjectives used to describe black and white basketball and football players. He found that whites were most often described with adjectives that referred to their "brains," while black players were described by their "brawn." "Many people want to believe that the success of African American athletes is somehow natural and physical, even genetic," says author Farai Chideya. "They do not choose to take into account the perseverance, skill, training, constant practice, and dedication of so many black athletes, particularly given the appeal of professional sports as a dream route out of poverty."[45]

Advertising in multicultural America

Advertisers too have increasingly realized the buying power and influence of America's diverse racial and ethnic groups. They have targeted these groups to both pitch and sell their products. "What is considered 'all American' has changed," said one corporate spokesperson. "The most all-American brand is the most inclusive brand."[46] Companies selling services such as banking or long-distance telephone plans portray ethnic and racial minorities in positive social interactions, working productively or engaging in family life. Meanwhile, minority celebrities, sports stars, and hip-hop artists appear in print and television ads to endorse everything from sneakers to credit cards.

Some companies try to boost their profits by appealing directly to minority ethnic groups. AT&T, for example, spent millions of dollars to attract Asian American and Latino customers who often call relatives and friends outside of the United States. Major toy companies have introduced multicultural figures, including African American, Latino, and even Muslim Barbie dolls and GI Joes.

Sometimes reaching new immigrants means marketing in their native languages. Many firms create separate commercials for Spanish-language television giants Univision or Telemundo, as well as Asian-language TV and newspapers. Often it is not enough to just translate the ads into Spanish, Korean, or Chinese. Advertisers must also understand subtle cultural differences. A Pepsi ad campaign, for example, that invited people to "come alive" by drinking Pepsi translated literally in Chinese to "bring your ancestors back from the dead."[47] To avoid making rude or embarrassing mistakes, consumer product companies hire consultants and conduct surveys and focus groups with minority consumers.

Corporations spend huge amounts of money to market products across racial lines because it makes good business sense. Minority consumers in America are estimated to have a buying power of more than $1 trillion annually. They represent one-quarter of the nation's current population. Corporate marketers say that projecting an image of diversity makes companies seem young, urban, and forward looking.

Yet the new multicultural advertising does not always accurately reflect corporate reality. Many of the same companies that are successful as ethnic marketers struggle to resolve racist policies in their own workplaces. Stores that try to present a multicultural image may engage in racial profiling of the African Americans and Latinos who shop there. Banks that portray black families using their services may discriminate against minority clients and small businesses in their mortgage or loan policies. Indeed, some corporations have used multicultural advertising campaigns to repair a tarnished public image. In one corporate image ad launched by Texaco in 1998, for example, a black petroleum explorer leads a team through a hazardous sandstorm and later says, "Don't you just love this job?"[48] Just two years earlier, Texaco was found to be actively discriminating against minority employees and settled a race-discrimination suit for a record $176 million.

Youth at the forefront of cultural change

Advertisers are most likely to project an inclusive, multicultural image as they try to market products that appeal to young Americans. This is because young people often cross racial and ethnic boundaries in their music and television preferences, fashion, and language. In part, this is a reflection of America's changing demographics. There are currently more multiracial young people than at any other time in U.S. history, and more young people with immigrant parents than any generation in the past eighty years.

But the changes are not just about demographics. Young people are at the forefront in changing attitudes about race and culture in America. James U. McNeal, an expert on the children's consumer market, explains that young people have "watched *Sesame Street* with adults and children of every race, had schoolmates increasingly from Mexico,

Diverse television characters like those on Sesame Street *have helped younger Americans become more comfortable with a multiethnic society.*

from Vietnam, from India. Their textbooks emphasize multiculturalism. And they've spent more time away from their parents, in day care and after-school care or home alone, so peer influence and these other forces are stronger."[49] In short, young people tend not to want to be held to traditional ideas about racial and ethnic identity if it limits whom they can associate with or how they should act.

Even as the major networks struggle with issues of diversity in their adult programming, cable television shows for young audiences have led the way in breaking down racial stereotypes and casting actors without regard to race. Stations such as Nickelodeon and MTV that focus entirely on the youth market broadcast shows with culturally diverse characters and themes. Television executives say that when they conduct group interviews to measure viewers' reactions to new shows, young people are less likely than adults to be concerned about or even mention the race of the characters. "They [young people] accept what they see on the screen with fewer biases and defenses,"[50] one network executive explains.

One effect of this increased cultural openness among the youngest generation is that attitudes toward once-taboo social practices such as interracial dating have become more relaxed. In a 1997 *USA Today*/Gallup poll, 57 percent of high school students who date said they had gone out with someone of another race or ethnic group, up from 17 percent in 1980. While some parents may still warn their children that dating someone of another race is unacceptable, young people are exposed to media images every day that contradict this view. Commercials, music videos, and television programs show interracial friends and couples dancing, relaxing, and enjoying the products and lifestyles that young people find most appealing. The message these images send is that interracial relationships are definitely OK.

Young people are also more accepting of multiracial or mixed-race Americans than the members of their parents' generation. There are a growing number of multiracial student organizations on college campuses and in high schools, as well as Web sites, chat rooms, and magazines devoted entirely to issues of concern to multiethnic or multiracial Americans. In the past, children of interracial marriages often faced external pressure to choose to identify with one of their parents' backgrounds and reject the other. Today, many young people take pride in their mixed racial heritage and refuse to be labeled in an either/or way.

Young Americans who are not multiracial themselves are likely to have a friend who is, or to count among their heroes one of a growing number of multiracial sports stars, actors, and musicians. Champion golfer Tiger Woods

Although young Americans embrace multiracial celebrity figures like golfer Tiger Woods, racial and ethnic discrimination remains a significant problem in the United States.

is one of the most famous of a generation of multiracial young Americans who are helping to change the rigid ways in which many people have traditionally thought about race.

Woods burst on the national scene in 1997 with his record-setting victory at the American Masters golf tournament. Because his skin color appears to be that of an African American, Woods's win was touted in the media as a sign of racial progress for blacks in a sport that had long been dominated by whites. But Woods refused to be pigeonholed. In an interview soon after his historic win, he told national talk show host Oprah Winfrey, "Growing up I came up with this name. I'm a Cablinasian." He explained that this was a term he had invented for Caucasian, black, Indian, and Asian to reflect the backgrounds of both of his parents. "I'm just who I am,"[51] he told Winfrey.

Does popular culture change attitudes?

While American youths may be willing to embrace African American rap artists or Latino sports heroes, these changes do not necessarily reflect a growing commitment to improved racial or ethnic relations in the country. Members of this generation were born after the civil rights movement of the 1960s and have grown up without formal barriers to racial equality. They have become more accepting of interracial dating and marriage, for example. But on social issues such as racial segregation, they still hold many of the same values and attitudes as their parents. An MTV poll in 1997 found that a majority of young people ages fifteen to twenty-four see nothing wrong with the races remaining separate from one another as long as everyone somehow has equal opportunities. Their attitudes toward discrimination and racial profiling are also similar to their parents' views and just as often divided along racial lines. Young people are also among the most likely members of American society to commit hate crimes, which have remained at steady levels over the past decade.

At the same time, it is young Americans who have been the first to fully accept a popular culture that reflects the nation's diversity, and this may signal deeper changes in the way they think about race and ethnicity.

Although it is too early to tell if these changes will translate into something more meaningful, it is clear that the way Americans think of themselves and the image of the country they project to the world is dramatically changing. In the nation's popular and commercial culture, the new face of America is truly multicultural.

Notes

Chapter 1: The Changing Face of the Nation

1. Mary M. Kent et al., "First Glimpses from the 2000 U.S. Census," *Population Bulletin,* June 2001, p. 26. www.prb.org.

2. Nathan Glazer, "Do We Need the Census Race Question?" *Public Interest,* Fall 2002, p. 22.

3. Quoted in Kent et al., "First Glimpses from the 2000 U.S. Census," p. 42, box 6.

4. Ellis Cose, *Color-Blind: Seeing Beyond Race in a Race-Obsessed World.* New York: Harper Perennial, 1997, p. 5.

5. Quoted in Richard N. Ostling, "In So Many Gods We Trust," *Time,* January 30, 1995.

6. Gustav Niebuhr, "Across America, Immigration Is Changing the Face of Religion," *New York Times,* September 23, 1999, p. A18.

7. Quoted in Richard N. Ostling, "The Intermarriage Quandary: Can U.S. Judaism Afford to Say Yes? Can It Afford Not To?" *Time,* October 3, 1988.

8. William H. Frey, *Metro Magnets for Minorities and Whites: Melting Pots, the New Sunbelt, and the Heartland.* Ann Arbor, MI: Population Studies Center, 2002, p. 7. www.psc.isr.umich.edu/pubs.

9. Quoted in Rob Paral, *Immigrants of the Heartland: How Immigration Is Revitalizing America's Midwest.* Chicago: Illinois Coalition for Immigrant and Refugee Rights, 2000, p. 15. www.icirr.org.

10. Quoted in Joan Montgomery Halford, "A Different Mirror: A Conversation with Ronald Takaki," *Educational Leadership,* April 1999, p. 8.

11. Linda Chavez, "Multiculturalism Is Driving Us Apart," *USA Today Magazine,* May 1996, p. 45.

Chapter 2: America's Racial and Ethnic Tensions

12. *Economist,* "The New Americans: Yes, They'll Fit In Too," May 11, 1991.

13. Quoted in Otto Friedrich, "The Changing Face of America," *Time,* July 8, 1985.

14. Steve Liss, "America's Immigrant Challenge," *Time Special Issue: The New Face of America,* Fall 1993, p. 4.

15. Quoted in American Psychological Association, "Hate Crimes Today: An Age-Old Foe in Modern Dress," 1998. www.apa.org.

16. Shashi Tharoor, "Letter from America: Racial Intolerance Increases in United States After Terrorist Attacks," *Newsweek International,* October 29, 2001, p. 61.

17. Quoted in Diana L. Eck, *A New Religious America: How a "Christian Country" Has Become the World's Most Religiously Diverse Nation.* San Francisco: Harper San Francisco, 2001, p. 229.

18. Cose, *Color-Blind,* p. 187.

19. Carol M. Swain, *The New White Nationalism in America: Its Challenge to Integration.* Cambridge, England: Cambridge University Press, 2002, p. 6.

20. City Year. www.cityyear.org.

21. Quoted in Serge Schmemann, "Us and Them: The Burden of Tolerance in a World of Division," *New York Times,* December 29, 2002, section 4, p. 1.

22. Quoted in American Friends Service Committee, "Understanding Anti-Immigrant Movements." www.afsc.org.

Chapter 3: Racial and Ethnic Discrimination

23. Quoted in Emilia Askari, "Profiling: Scouts Detained After Trip to Island," *Detroit Free Press,* October 13, 2001.

24. Quoted in Askari, "Profiling: Scouts Detained After Trip to Island."

25. U.S. Constitution, amend. 14, sec. 1.

26. *Civil Rights Act of 1964,* Public Law 88-352, 88th Cong. (July 2, 1964), sec. 201(a).

27. Kenneth Meeks, *Driving While Black: What to Do If You Are a Victim of Racial Profiling.* New York: Broadway Books, 2000, p. 89.

28. Quoted in Cose, *Color-Blind,* p. 159.

29. U.S. Equal Employment Opportunity Commission, "Federal Laws Prohibiting Job Discrimination Questions and Answers." www.eeoc.gov/facts/qanda.html.

30. Quoted in Randall Kennedy, "Race, the Police, and 'Reasonable Suspicion,'" presentation to the National Institute of Justice, Washington, D.C., February 1998, p. 2.

31. Randall Kennedy, "Suspect Policy: Racial Profiling Usually Isn't Racist; It Can Help Stop Crime; and It Should Be Abolished," *New Republic,* September 13, 1999, p. 32.

32. Quoted in Kennedy, "Race, the Police, and 'Reasonable Suspicion,'" p. 4.

33. Kennedy, "Race, the Police, and 'Reasonable Suspicion,'" p. 5.

34. Quoted in Street Law and the Supreme Court Historical Society, "Comparing the University of California at Davis's Admissions Program to Harvard's." *Regents of the University of California v. Bakke (1978).* www.landmarkcases.org.

Chapter 4: Educating a Diverse Generation

35. Quoted in Todd Gitlin, *The Twilight of Common Dreams: Why America Is Wracked by Culture Wars.* New York: Metropolitan Books, 1995, p. 19.

36. Quoted in Halford, "A Different Mirror: A Conversation with Ronald Takaki," pp. 17–20.

37. Linda Chavez, "Rich Liberals Versus the Poor," *Conservative News and Information,* October 2, 2002. www.townhall.com.

Chapter 5: Media and Popular Culture in a Multicultural Society

38. Farai Chideya, "A Nation of Minorities: America in 2050," *Civil Rights Journal,* Fall 1999, p. 35.

94

39. Children Now, "New Study Finds Children See Inequities in Media's Race and Class Portrayals," Children Now press release, May 6, 1998. www.childrennow.org.

40. Farai Chideya, *Don't Believe the Hype: Fighting Cultural Misinformation About African-Americans.* New York: Plume, 1995, p. xiii.

41. Quoted in Alan James Frutkin, "Television/Radio: The Faces in the Glass Are Rarely Theirs," *New York Times,* December 24, 2000, p. 31.

42. Quoted in Frutkin, "Television/Radio: The Faces in the Glass Are Rarely Theirs," p. 31.

43. Quoted in Leon E. Wynter, *American Skin: Pop Culture, Big Business, and the End of White America.* New York: Crown, 2002, p. 102.

44. Quoted in Tim Wendel, *The New Face of Baseball: The One-Hundred-Year Rise and Triumph of Latinos in America's Favorite Sport.* New York: HarperCollins, 2003, p. 180.

45. Chideya, *Don't Believe the Hype,* p. 155.

46. Quoted in Wynter, *American Skin,* p. 140.

47. Bert Eljera, "Target Asian America: Savvy Marketers Are Scrambling for a Piece of the APA Pie," *Asian Week,* December 6–13, 1996.

48. Quoted in Wynter, *American Skin.,* p. 163.

49. Quoted in Dale Russakoff, "Keeping Up with the Garcias," *Washington Post,* September 23, 2000, p. A1.

50. Quoted in Russakoff, "Keeping Up with the Garcias," p. A1.

51. Quoted in Gary Kamiya, "Cablinasian Like Me: Tiger Woods' Rejection of Orthodox Racial Classifications Points the Way to a Future Where Race Will No Longer Define Us." *Salon,* April 1997, p. 2. www.salon.com/april97/tiger970430.html.

Organizations
to Contact

American Civil Liberties Union (ACLU)
125 Broad St., 18th Floor
New York, NY 10004
www.aclu.org

The ACLU is a national organization that works to actively promote and defend the liberties and civil rights of all Americans.

American Immigration Law Foundation (AILF)
918 F St., 6th Floor
Washington, DC 20004
(202) 742-5600
www.ailf.org

AILF is a pro-immigration organization that works to increase public understanding of immigration policies and promote fairness under the law for immigrant groups.

Bureau of Citizenship and Immigration Services
425 I St. NW
Washington, DC 20536
(202) 514-2837
http://uscis.gov

The Bureau of Citizenship and Immigration Services provides immigration services and processes immigrant visas and citizenship applications.

The Pluralism Project
Harvard University
201 Vanserg Hall
25 Francis Ave.
Cambridge, MA 02138
(617) 496-2481
www.fas.harvard.edu/~pluralism

The Pluralism Project studies and documents America's growing religious diversity. The Web site includes images of immigrant religious communities across the United States and provides access to the project's publications. A teacher's resource section also provides information and links for students.

For Further Reading

Books

Farai Chideya, *The Color of Our Future.* New York: William Morrow, 1999. Explores the impact of America's demographic changes on the nation's future. The author recounts her experiences as she travels across the country to profile young people and their attitudes about race.

Ellis Cose, *Color-Blind: Seeing Beyond Race in a Race-Obsessed World.* New York: Harper Perennial, 1997. An African American *Newsweek* columnist explores Americans' perceptions of race and controversial issues such as affirmative action.

Pearl Fuyo Gaskins, *What Are You? Voices of Mixed Race Young People.* New York: Henry Holt, 1999. Interviews with multiracial young people from diverse backgrounds about their personal experiences. Also includes poetry, personal writings, and a list of multimedia resources for those wishing to explore the topic further.

Jenna Weissman Joselit, *Immigration and American Religion.* Oxford, England: Oxford University Press, 2001. A historical overview of immigrant religions for young adult readers, with chapters devoted to Christianity, Judaism, and Asian religions.

Ronald Takaki, *Strangers at the Gates Again: Asian American Immigration After 1965.* New York: Chelsea House, 1995. Takaki is a proponent of multiculturalism who has written extensively about Asian American history. In this book for young adult readers, he recounts the experiences of the latest wave of immigrants from Asia.

Mary E. Williams, ed., *Interracial America: Opposing Viewpoints.* San Diego: Greenhaven Press, 2001. Designed for young adult readers, this is a collection of articles and commentaries representing different sides of controversial issues such as racial identity, immigration, affirmative action, and interracial marriage.

Web Sites

City Year (www.cityyear.org). City Year is a non-profit organization that works to unite young people of diverse backgrounds in volunteer service to their communities. The Web site describes the group's mission and programs, and how to become involved.

Facing History and Ourselves (www.facinghistory.org). This Web site includes readings, Web links, and student projects on civil rights and overcoming prejudice.

The New Americans (www.pbs.org/newamericans). The Web site is designed to accompany a public television (PBS) series that profiles new immigrants to America. It includes immigrant stories, background information, and a link to a sample citizenship test.

U.S. Census Bureau (www.census.gov). The Census Bureau's extensive Web site includes *Gateway to Census 2000,* with articles, charts, maps, and sample surveys that break down the U.S. population by race, ethnicity, and other measures. In the section for teachers, there is a history of census taking, sample forms, and charts and maps for use by students.

Works Consulted

Books

Stephen L. Carter, *Reflections of an Affirmative Action Baby.* New York: BasicBooks, 1991. Drawing on his own experiences, the author takes a close look at the controversy over affirmative action and considers its future.

Farai Chideya, *Don't Believe the Hype: Fighting Cultural Misinformation About African-Americans.* New York: Plume, 1995. Looks at stereotypes and misperceptions about African Americans that are perpetuated in the media.

Ellis Cose, *A Nation of Strangers: Prejudice, Politics, and the Populating of America.* New York: Wiliam Morrow, 1992. A look at the controversial politics of immigration and race in America.

Diana L. Eck, *A New Religious America: How a "Christian Country" Has Become the World's Most Religiously Diverse Nation.* San Francisco: Harper San Francisco, 2001. An account of the new religious diversity in America and its effect on the nation's religious life.

Todd Gitlin, *The Twilight of Common Dreams: Why America Is Wracked by Culture Wars.* New York: Metropolitan Books, 1995. An analysis of the "culture wars" and multiculturalism in education.

Kenneth Meeks, *Driving While Black: What to Do If You Are a Victim of Racial Profiling.* New York: Broadway Books, 2000. The author describes incidents of racial profiling and discusses the ways in which Americans can take action to stop them.

Gary B. Nash, Charlotte Crabtree, and Ross E. Dunn, *History on Trial: Culture Wars and the Teaching of the Past.* New York:

Alfred A. Knopf, 1997. The authors are proponents of multiculturalism who were involved in the California history textbook debate.

Arthur M. Schlesinger Jr., *The Disuniting of America: Reflections on a Multicultural Society.* New York: W.W. Norton, 1991. Pulitzer Prize–winning historian Arthur Schlesinger Jr. considers what it means to be an American in a multicultural society.

Carol M. Swain, *The New White Nationalism in America: Its Challenge to Integration.* Cambridge, England: Cambridge University Press, 2002. A political scientist examines the "new white nationalist movement" and explores how it is fueled by growing frustration with affirmative action and multiculturalism.

Tim Wendel, *The New Face of Baseball: The One-Hundred-Year Rise and Triumph of Latinos in America's Favorite Sport.* New York: HarperCollins, 2003. Profiles Latino baseball players and their influence on the game.

Leon E. Wynter, *American Skin: Pop Culture, Big Business, and the End of White America.* New York: Crown, 2002. A lively analysis of the rise of a new American popular and commercial culture that crosses racial and ethnic boundaries.

Periodicals
Emilia Askari, "Profiling: Scouts Detained After Trip to Island," *Detroit Free Press,* October 13, 2001.

Dan Baum, "Patriots on the Borderline; Toting Guns, Cameras, and Mighty Convictions, Small Bands of Americans Are Patrolling the Southwest in Search of Illegal Immigrants," *Los Angeles Times,* March 16, 2003.

Linda Chavez, "Multiculturalism Is Driving Us Apart," *USA Today Magazine,* May 1996.

Farai Chideya, "A Nation of Minorities: America in 2050," *Civil Rights Journal*, Fall 1999.

Tammerlin Drummond, "It's Not Just in New Jersey: Cops Across the U.S. Often Search People Just Because of Their Race, a Study Says," *Time,* June 14, 1999.

Economist, "The New Americans: Yes, They'll Fit in Too," May 11, 1991.

Bert Eljera, "Target Asian Americans: Savvy Marketers Are Scrambling for a Piece of the APA Pie," *Asian Week,* December 6–13, 1996.

Christopher John Farley, "Hip-Hop Nation: There's More to Rap than Just Rhythms and Rhymes. After Two Decades, It Has Transformed the Culture of America," *Time,* February 8, 1999.

Otto Friedrich, "The Changing Face of America," *Time,* July 8, 1985.

Alan James Frutkin, "Television/Radio: The Faces in the Glass Are Rarely Theirs," *New York Times,* December 24, 2000.

Paul Gagnon, "Why Study History?" *Atlantic Monthly,* November 1988.

Nancy Gibbs, "Shades of Difference: Immigrants Are Building an Ethnic Mosaic, but the Pieces Don't Quite Fit Together," *Time,* November 18, 1991.

Nathan Glazer, "Do We Need the Census Race Question?" *Public Interest,* Fall 2002.

Paul Gray, "Whose America? A Growing Emphasis on the Nation's 'Multicultural' Heritage Exalts Racial and Ethnic Pride at the Expense of Social Cohesion," *Time,* July 8, 1991.

Joan Montgomery Halford, "A Different Mirror: A Conversation with Ronald Takaki," *Educational Leadership,* April 1999.

K. Connie Kang and Lisa Richardson, "Legacy of the Riots: 1992–2002," *Los Angeles Times,* April 27, 2002.

Randall Kennedy, "Race, the Police, and 'Reasonable Suspicion.'" Presentation to the National Institute of Justice, Washington, D.C., February 1998.

————, "Suspect Policy: Racial Profiling Usually Isn't Racist; It Can Help Stop Crime; and It Should Be Abolished," *New Republic,* September 13, 1999.

Knight Ridder/Tribune News Service, "Latinos Hardly Visible on Prime-Time Television, UCLA Study Finds," November 29, 1994.

Adam Liptak, "Diversity's Precarious Moorings," *New York Times,* December 8, 2002.

Steve Liss, "America's Immigrant Challenge," *Time Special Issue: The New Face of America,* Fall 1993.

Charlie McCollum, "Nickelodeon Presents a Loving Latino Family on 'Brothers Garcia,'" Knight Ridder/Tribune News Service, July 12, 2000.

Dana Milbank and Emily Wax, "Bush Visits Mosque to Forestall Hate Crimes," *Washington Post,* September 18, 2001.

Gustav Niebuhr, "Across America, Immigration Is Changing the Face of Religion," *New York Times,* September 23, 1999.

Richard N. Ostling, "In So Many Gods We Trust," *Time,* January 30, 1995.

————, "The Intermarriage Quandary: Can U.S. Judaism Afford to Say Yes? Can It Afford Not To?" *Time,* October 3, 1988.

James Poniewozik, "What's Wrong with This Picture? The U.S. Hispanic Population Has Grown 58% in 10 Years, to 35 Million. On TV, Latinos Are Down to 2% of Characters. Why the Brownout?" *Time,* May 29, 2001.

Dale Russakoff, "Keeping Up with the Garcias," *Washington Post,* September 23, 2000.

Serge Schmemann, "Us and Them: The Burden of Tolerance in a World of Division," *New York Times,* December 29, 2002.

Shawnee News-Star, "MTV Poll Finds More Youth Accept 'Separate but Equal' Concept," December 5, 1997.

Gloria Stewner-Manzanares, "The Bilingual Education Act: Twenty Years Later," *New Focus,* Fall 1988.

Shashi Tharoor, "Letter from America: Racial Intolerance Increases in United States After Terrorist Attacks," *Newsweek International,* October 29, 2001.

Rob Walker, "Whassup Barbie? Marketers Are Embracing the Idea of a 'Post-Racial' America. Goodbye, Niche Marketing," *Boston Globe,* January 12, 2003.

Jack E. White, "'I'm Just Who I Am': White Black Asian Other Race Is No Longer as Simple as Black or White. So, What Does This Mean for America?" *Time,* May 5, 1997.

Internet Sources

American Friends Service Committee, "Understanding Anti-Immigrant Movements." www.afsc.org.

American Psychological Association, "Hate Crimes Today: An Age-Old Foe in Modern Dress," 1998. www.apa.org.

Linda Chavez, "Rich Liberals Versus the Poor," *Conservative News and Information,* October 2, 2002. www.townhall.com.

Children Now, "New Study Finds Children See Inequities in Media's Race and Class Portrayals," Children Now press release, May 6, 1998. www.childrennow.org.

Federal Bureau of Investigation (FBI), "Hate Crime Statistics," 2001. www.fbi.gov/ucr/ucr.htm.

William H. Frey, *Metro Magnets for Minorities and Whites: Melting Pots, the New Sunbelt, and the Heartland.* Ann Arbor, MI: Population Studies Center, 2002. www.psc.isr. umich.edu/pubs.

———, "The United States Population: Where the New Immigrants Are," *Electronic Journal of the United States Information Agency,* June 1999. http://usinfo.state.gov/ journals/itsv/0699/ijse/frey.htm.

Gary Kamiya, "Cablinasian Like Me: Tiger Woods' Rejection of Orthodox Racial Classifications Points the Way to a Future

Where Race Will No Longer Define Us," *Salon,* April 1997. www.salon.com/april97/tiger970430.html.

Paul Kengor, *Evaluating World History Texts in Wisconsin Public High Schools.* Thiensville: Wisconsin Policy Research Institute, 2002. www.wpri.org.

Mary M. Kent et al., "First Glimpses from the 2000 U.S. Census," *Population Bulletin,* June 2001. www.prb.org.

Ontario Consultants on Religious Tolerance (OCRT), "Religions of the World." www.religioustolerance.org.

Rob Paral, *Immigrants of the Heartland: How Immigration Is Revitalizing America's Midwest.* Chicago: Illinois Coalition for Immigrant and Refugee Rights, 2000. www.icirr.org.

Pew Forum on Religion and Public Life, "Lift Every Voice: A Report on Religion in American Public Life," 2001. http://pewforum.org/religion.

Mark Potok, "Hate Takes a Hit as Deaths, Defections, Arrests, and Internal Splits Roil America's Embattled White Supremacist Movement," *Intelligence Report,* Spring 2003. www.splcenter.org.

Street Law and the Supreme Court Historical Society, "Comparing the University of California at Davis's Admissions Program to Harvard's." *Regents of the University of California v. Bakke (1978).* www.landmarkcases.org.

U.S. Department of Education, *Preventing Youth Hate Crime: A Manual for Schools and Communities.* www.ed.gov/pubs/ HateCrime/start.html.

U.S. Equal Employment Opportunity Commission, "Federal Laws Prohibiting Job Discrimination Questions and Answers." www.eeoc.gov/facts/qanda.html.

Index

Picture Credits

About the Author

Meryl Loonin is a writer who works on educational media projects. She has a background in documentary film and television production and a master's degree in education. She has produced and developed many film documentaries on topics such as human evolution, Latin American literature, life in the former Soviet Union, and the race to build the hydrogen bomb. Ms. Loonin also has a strong interest in helping young people publish their own work. She has collaborated on Web sites, videos, and books of creative work by and for kids. She lives in Lexington, Massachusetts, with her husband, Neil, and two children, Hana and Jonah.